Desperate Love
A Father's Memoir

Desperate Love
A Father's Memoir

by

Richard Reiss

Postscript by Paula Kaplan-Reiss, Ph.D.

SERVING HOUSE BOOKS

Desperate Love: A Father's Memoir

Copyright © 2011

All rights reserved.

ISBN: 978-0-9838289-1-4

Cover by Elyse Rosenberg

Author photo by Ethan Reiss

Serving House Books logo by Barry Lereng Wilmont

Published by Serving House Books, LLC

Copenhagen, Denmark and Florham Park, NJ

www.servinghousebooks.com

First Serving House Books Edition 2011

For Paula

With all my love

R

Prologue

Gabriel is gorgeous. By the time he is seven years old his physique is as ripped as an Olympic swimmer. He has taut muscles and a v-shaped upper body that define him as much as his wit, his humor and his unbearable stubbornness. But mostly it is that beautiful face, as wonderful as any baby on any package of diapers or baby food or baby wipes or baby shampoo. He is stunning. When you look at a child like him you are instantly struck by what appears to be a serene yet intense beauty, a beauty that is at once troublesome and confident—his dark complexion, his darker still eyes and his winsome ways make it impossible to not love a child like this, irrespective of what you think you know and what may surely follow. His beauty belies something deeper, an awful internal struggle that all troubled children confront. In their often chaotic worlds they are controlled by unknown demons; their very survival of mind and body is a daily struggle. This, it seems, is Gabriel—struggling, not knowing or being able to choose right over wrong. Yet he is so bright, so verbal, so smart and handsome. We see it all, (the struggle, the love, the conflict, the fear) but we tell ourselves that everything good is permanent and everything bad will pass with time. After all, he is so young; he will overcome his troubles...we will help him. This striking child will be a striking young man. His future is one of a survivor, a fighter—everything will be okay, everything will be fine. Gabriel is our blessing from God and God will look out for him and us. And that face (even at seven) will surely be worth something in a world where looks are important at all ages. Everyone sees it. Everyone says so. Gabriel is gorgeous.

Chapter 1

Our story was supposed to be ordinary—a simple life filled with the joys and tears and blessings that all normal lives encompass. But there is nothing ordinary to tell. The happy life that we craved was a perverse fantasy of two people who blithely accepted the obvious. Our plan was simple: first there was the wedding, then there were the children, and then there was the happiness forever and ever. That was what we thought, that was what our narrow experience in living told us: when all you desire is love, the world is a beautiful place. Children are perfect; they cuddle at night; they hug you. They accept and give love unconditionally. They depend on you for protection from everything large and small and bad in their world. But what happens when they don't? What happens when it is the parents who need protection from a child? What happens when the ordinary life, the simple life, is complex and frightening? Where is the love then? How does love sustain itself in a life consumed by fear?

I had a fantasy that went something like this: Little Bobby, Billy and Betty are lovely children. They are not great scholars, but they are smart enough. They are not the best looking children in the neighborhood, but they possess a sense of confidence that impresses adults and draws other children to them. When they are tired, they rest their weary bones on my sturdy body as I stroke their satin-like hair. When they are angry, we talk. When they are sad, I listen. When they do wrong, I am disappointed and my disappointment registers deep in their psyche. In the general scheme of a family, it's not just perfect, it's normal. Yet in reality, the life I have led has been the antithesis of my dreams. Love may be the glue, perhaps the only glue of which to make any sense of it all, but it is often a distant emotion buried beneath the realities of life with Gabriel. This story, my story… is deep, passionate, unyielding and imperfect. It is a story about faith and the undeniable belief in what is possible. It is a story about courage and hate and loneliness, and wanting to belong but not understanding how. My life is the story of my wife and three children. I am Rick. My wife is Paula, and I have three sons. Jonathan is my youngest. Ethan is in the middle. Gabriel is the eldest. This is Gabriel's story…my wonderful, magnificent, handsome and horrible son. I began this book when he was fifteen years old. I was sitting at my computer, and he was sitting in the family room watching television. It was a Friday night. It was 10:30 and he was in my house and speaking to my wife. It was a remarkably ordinary scene for a life that so far had been very distant from what was considered normal. Occasionally, I heard him laugh. It was a wonderful treat. In fact, it was amazing for a boy who less than a year earlier assured me that he would burn down my house. Who was this stranger who spoke to Paula and me on a Friday night? The zenith of his world, which had little to do with his family, was Friday nights at the Mall. Great bombs of disaster may have been falling, but this boy dressed in black pants and silver studded bracelets and leather neck ornaments and tattered hoodies to cover his eyes, would never miss his weekly pilgrimage to the smoke-filled outer perimeter of Macy's and J.C. Penny's and the multiplex theatre on each and every Friday night. It was his Mecca. It was where the disenfranchised youth of America, too old to stay at home and too young to drive, gathered in sinister clusters of youthful nothingness to the great disappointment of those who cared enough to worry.

This Friday, however, Gabriel was not at the mall. He was home from boarding school for a ten-day holiday. It was the longest period he had spent in our house since we had him kidnapped and taken to a therapeutic wilderness program nearly a year before. He had become more than we, or anyone we knew, could handle. He had found a group of alienated kids who were happy to replace us as his family. We had become superfluous and our home had become unlivable. Our house was too violent, too ugly. It was not a place where Gabriel could grow into the man of my fantasies. He was incredibly lost and so were we.

But now it's different. We hope it's different. There is a singular quality to our interactions that rarely existed before. He is civil. It's strange. There is an uneasy calm that, for the moment, suffuses the space between us. Is it real or is it Gabriel reluctantly abiding by the contract that sent him back to us? And what about the contract? He broke it. Once.

During his brief visit home he smoked a cigarette. Hardly a major offense in the eyes of some, particularly cast against his more serious crimes. Yet for a boy who lived a life without rules, a boy who lived every day in personal anarchy, living by the rules was his only future. When I confronted him, he denied it. Then, as if compelled to confess, he pulled an Ipod out of his jeans and a pack of matches fell to the ground.

I said to him, "I need to be able to trust you."

He said, "You can trust me. I am so much better now."

"I know you're better," I said. "But you still have a way to go."

"I'm ready," he said. "I'm ready to come home for good."

"No, you're not." And then I said, "Let's take a walk."

So we did. We walked for about a half hour and he tried desperately, as he had done many times before, to convince me that he was ready to come back and live with us again. He told me that the brainwashing he was going through at the Hidden Lake Academy therapeutic boarding school in Georgia wasn't working. He said that if we didn't let him stay home he would get in trouble as soon as he got back to school and we would be forced to send him to wilderness again. He said that if he had to go back to wilderness he would stay there until he reached eighteen, since he liked it better than school and knew that we couldn't afford to keep him there for very long (wilderness is $3,000 a week—school is $6,000 a month). And, by the way, when he completes the program at the therapeutic boarding school, in another eight months, he will not be completing high school. He had to make up for the lost years of his life and will mostly hang out with his friends, ride his bike, skateboard and smoke.

It was an amazing and wonderful conversation, as most of our conversations had been in recent months. He was, of course, delusional in his understanding of the world, desperately clinging to his subversive past. But not once did he curse. Not once did he raise his voice. Never did I feel physically threatened. And, as often happened when we talked about his life, he cried…briefly. His pleas, in fact, were getting a bit old and each time he began another recitation, he was less convincing. I guess the brainwashing was working…something was working. Slowly, painfully, he was returning to us.

●

Ours was not uncommon as fairy tales go. Step one was my aforementioned fantasy of a family. Step two was a couple very much in love. Step three was that same couple unable to bear children. They saw a world of babies and families and hopeful expectations and they were crushed by that which they could not possess: a baby of their own.

They were young. They were attractive. They were smart. They were us. So we began with infertility treatments. I learned how to give my wife shots and she learned how to create multiple eggs. Then she gets pregnant and miscarries. More shots, more eggs and more miscarriages. Three miscarriages and an ectopic pregnancy and we come to the realization that this isn't going as we had planned. But we were young and stupid, right? We were two relatively religious people that believed in God, but we never thought that God was sending us a message. What would that message be anyway? Sorry, kids, you don't deserve to be parents. Hey, Rick, remember that pack of gum you stole from the drug store when you were eight years old? Guess what? No children for you! God doesn't work like that, does He?

So what did we do? We ignored the spiritual signals emanating from my wife's miscarriages and dove further into an emotional and financial abyss. All we really wanted was for God to be our partner in helping us to create a life. Yet when it became brutally apparent that God was busy with the other six billion people on the planet, we decided to adopt. We were good people who had the potential to become affluent. Even if we weren't good and even if we never became affluent, we had so much love to give—tons of it—and wasn't that enough? Our love would shape a child regardless of its gene pool. Our love, more powerful than our pain, would be more than any baby would need for a happy and fulfilling life.

A mere year after we had begun the process of adoption, hardly longer than a normal pregnancy, we had a baby in our home. He was healthy and beautiful and ours. It was hard to imagine two people, on this planet or any other, that could remotely mirror our daily euphoria.

I wrote about him often, this amazing son of mine. He was (and still is) my muse. During the early years of his life, there was nothing he did that was short of brilliant. I wrote. I wondered. I prayed until I realized that the prayers that mattered most seemed only to matter to me.

To be honest, however, the first few years of Gabriel's life were nothing short of magical. Our son was a charming, handsome and intelligent child that was adored not only by his formerly desperate parents, but by all those who came in contact with him. He had presence and personality and he was so much fun. By the time he was one, he was coy and playful and engaging with family and friends alike. And he was, lest we forget, a uniquely beautiful baby boy. Dark complexion. Dark wonderful eyes. Hair, the color of waxed cherry wood. He was a child whose laughter was magnetic. It engulfed you and surrounded your heart with joy.

I remember this because I force myself. I remember this when the guy who is replacing my windshield asks me how it broke and I tell him that a rock from a truck on the highway flew up and hit it. I embellished the story and I said, "God, it was so loud that I thought someone had shot a gun or something." He was smarter than me though, and he smiled and said, "Yeah, that can be really scary," even though he could see it was broken from the inside. But I said nothing, not wanting to share my son's uncontrollable rage or my own feelings of guilt. It was just another cover-up, another story for me to bury and someday forget.

Chapter 2

For months he rides his little red bike with one training wheel. He doesn't need it, but like the blanket he sleeps with every night, it makes him feel safe. I know I shouldn't care, (what's a training wheel after all) but I want him to be fearless like me when I was his age and a training wheel ruins that image. Nearly every day I ask him if today is the day I can take it off. I'm kind. I'm gentle. I'm cajoling. I'm getting nowhere.

One day, I just do it. I find my wrench and remove the bracket that holds the wheel in place. With the training wheel removed, there is nothing to lean on. Gabriel would have to muster up some seven-year-old determination if he wanted to continue to enjoy the freedoms of two-wheeled transportation.

When he discovers the missing wheel, he is not happy. I said, "Gabriel, let's go for a ride together. You don't need a training wheel. You're great at riding your bike. Come on…time for you to take a chance."

"I'll fall," he said, in a voice that is sweet and tender and nervous.

"No you won't."

Two weeks go by and he hasn't gone near his bike. Paula thinks I should put the wheel back on. "I'm telling you," I said. "He'll do it. I know this boy."

Another week passes and still he refuses to ride the bike despite the many offers I make to go with him. And then one day, as I am coming home from work, there is Gabriel riding in the street. He wears a black helmet with yellow lightning bolts. He moves swiftly in perpendicular motion to the ground: clasping the handle bars, looking ahead, and beaming as if he had just won the Tour de France.

My sense of pride was overwhelming. He did it. He figured it out. He learned that a little determination goes a long way. "Yo! Gabriel! You did it," I screamed from my car window. And he turned to look at me. And he kept on peddling. And he disappeared around the corner.

●

Gabriel climbs into our bed late at night when he can't sleep. "Rub my back," he says. "Please." It's an innocent request fraught with longing; it's a plea like a dog that forces his head under your hand desperate for a human connection.

So Paula rubs his back. She does it because she loves him. She does it because she knows that a moment as rare as this will surely fade with time. The lights are dim; I am nearly asleep. He's her baby and he needs her. "What's the matter, sweetie?" she says. "I can't sleep," he quietly replies.

He puts his head in her lap as her hand slowly, methodically, moves across his back. He is not thinking about his day or about the fight with his brother or even about the trouble at school. He is thinking about sleep and wishing he could. He wants a pill, maybe that will help, but I hate to give him another pill for anything. "Too many pills already and none of them are working." That's what I say. So he closes his eyes and falls into the moment. His mother's hand, soft as cotton, warms him.

Paula feels his breath through her nightshirt. It's heavy and moist and wonderful, and for the moment she is not lost in her anger or her sadness. She is his mother and she hums to him.

Twenty minutes pass; Gabriel is still awake. "Come on, baby. I'll walk you to bed," she says. So together they walk down the hall, their arms wrapped around each other. Gabriel climbs into bed and Paula pulls the covers up and over the shoulders that for the last twenty minutes she gently massaged. "Sweet dreams," she says, and kisses him on the forehead. "Good night, Mommy," says Gabriel.

"Gabe, can I turn out the light?" she asks.

"No, leave it on."

For all his bravura he is not a risk-taker. He has never jumped out of a window or tried to cross the highway. He is not drawn to adventurous things. He does not like roller coasters or mountain climbing or river rafting. We take comfort in knowing that this is one thing we don't have to worry about. Not yet. The wildness, the anger, the emerging violence, has been restricted to our home.

It's nearly noon when Gabriel wakes up. He showers, eats and is gone. Like a dandelion seed caught in the wind he floats from house to house and friend to friend. He is a waif looking for a meal or a bed or a family to love him. He is not even twelve years old, but rarely is he home. He is constantly, relentlessly, endlessly begging to stay at a friend's. It's a new phenomena but troubling nonetheless. Who are the friends? Who are the parents? What's going on?

At six p.m. the phone rings. It's Gabriel. "Dad," he says, "I'm going to sleep at Brandon's tonight, okay?" Brandon is a new name in the growing repertoire of friends and so now the struggle is how to answer the question to avoid the battle. It's a no-win situation.

"I don't know Brandon," I say. "I don't know where he lives. I don't know his parents. It's time to come home for dinner, Gabe."

"I am eating at Brandon's," he says.

"Okay, let me talk to his parents," I respond.

"They're not home," he says, and it's back and forth until finally and sternly I say, "Gabriel, I want you home for dinner!"

"You suck!" shouts Gabriel, and hangs up the phone.

Soon he is home. I hear him. He dismounts his bike, throws it against the garage wall, and does not watch as it hits a shovel, a rake, a tennis racquet, and another bicycle, all of which fall to the ground. The house door opens and slams and without a word Gabriel heads for the basement to bang on his drums.

A year ago we gave him a drum set. He seems to have a predisposition, if not a need for it. In moments of crises, such as this might become, Gabriel often takes to playing his drums. He understands beat and rhythm and has very agile hands. Even when he isn't upset, he often plays long and loud just as he is doing now. The truth is, he isn't all that bad, and the drums provide a necessary and appropriate outlet for his boundless energy and anger. On this night, however, they are not enough.

Ten minutes pass and he emerges from the basement. "I want to go to Brandon's," he says.

"Daddy already said no, Gabe. We are not going to let you stay with strangers," says Paula.

"He's not a stranger. He's my friend."

"If he's your friend, how come we've never met him?" I ask.

"You don't know all my friends and I don't want you to know *any* of them," he blurts out.

"Stay home," I implore. "We'll watch a movie."

"This is bullshit," says Gabriel, who only recently developed the courage to curse in front of us.

He walks out. He slams the door and I follow. We look at each other for a moment, father and son, probing each other's eyes. There was a time when I could look in those eyes and feel a nearly incomprehensible love. More than just his physical beauty or his mere presence in my house, it was a bond between two different but like-minded people in search of each other. We found each other and it was glorious, but that too is surely fading with Gabriel's imminent adolescence. At the moment, however, he is too angry to think, but I am not. I catch his gaze—briefly—instantly—his deep black pearl eyes nestled in a face the color of honey. *Will it ever stop*, I think. *Will it ever stop*?

"I have to go," pleads Gabriel.

"I'm sorry, Gabe. No," I say as I go back into the house.

I pray that it's over but experience tells me otherwise. Gabriel will be back. He will be in my face, relentless to the point of frightening. Worse case, we will call the police. Second worse case, we will leave the house. Third worse case, we will lock him out of the house until he calms down. All three possibilities make me sick to my stomach.

Jonathan, who is seven, will be terrified and I will tell him to stay in his room where Gabriel will not bother him. Ethan, who is nine, will also be scared, but he will offer a suggestion. "Just do it," he will say. "Just take him to his friend's." Ethan, like me, does not like conflict.

The ensuing fight is sure to harden me and I know it. I know that it won't come down to right or wrong or trust or knowing Brandon or his parents. It will devolve into winning, and whether or not, on this occasion, I want to let my eleven-year-old boy win. I will try to remember in my anger that what I want most is to protect Gabriel. It's always about Gabriel; it's never about me. Not yet. I love him too much.

Soon it's dark. There's a summer fog settling early in the evening. It's not so thick but thick enough to hide a tree or a boy on his bike.

"Take me to Brandon's," says Gabriel.

"No," I say yet again.

"Take me to Brandon's!" he screams, and now he punches the door with such ferocity that I can hear it crack.

"Stop it, Gabe!" I scream as I grab his wrist. And for a second, maybe two, there is a struggle. Gabriel frees himself, bolts out the door, jumps on his bike and is gone.

It's over in an instant. The damage was minimal, but what do I do now?

"Don't worry, Paula," I say. "He won't go far."

She knows I'm right but almost wishes I was wrong. If I were wrong then all we would have to do is worry. If I were wrong than all we would have to do is figure out who Brandon is.

Thirty minutes later and Gabriel is back. His face is wet from the fog which makes him look as if he were crying. It's a sympathetic face; it makes him more human. He repeats his plea, "Take me to Brandon's, please!"

"Gabriel," says Paula, "It's late. If he really wanted you to sleep over, don't you think he would have called by now?"

And he does it again. "I hate you," he screams and punches the door as ferociously as before. And once again I hear it crack. And this time there is a small indentation from his knuckle. And he flies out the door because not doing so would cause him to explode.

This beautiful child—this angel—this boy I call my son is slipping through the spaces between my fingers. He is acid and my hands are burning.

"Shit," I howl, forcing out the word slowly and painfully, dragging it along as if doing so will ease the reality of the situation. And I say it again, and again, and again. "Shit!"

Gabriel peddles fast. I'm sure he feels the fog, thicker now, collecting on his brow, his nose, and his cheeks. Is he nervous riding in the dark? Probably, but he is determined.

Later, I learn that it's not very far to Brandon's house, but there are two heavily trafficked roads to cross to get into his development, roads that Gabriel has never crossed alone before. I know what he is thinking. I am sure of it. *What an asshole I am*, he must be saying to himself. *Why did I ever go home? I hate my parents. I'll do whatever I want.* And then, alone in his thoughts, he surely has the epiphany I feared most. His anger has empowered him to overcome his fears. When he gets to the first road and he sees the cars whizzing by, he nonetheless crosses. And when he gets to the other road and he sees all the other cars, each one speeding past a stationary boy on a yellow bike, he crosses that one too. I'm only a few hundred feet behind him. We live in a small town and it's not hard to find a kid on his bike at eleven o'clock in the evening. When I spot him I decide not to force him to come home. I'm proud of my detective work, and follow him over roads number one and two as he slowly makes his way to Brandon's house.

It's remarkable that Gabriel hasn't seen me, hasn't realized that the light that is following him is me. He is singularly focused and anything short of exploding fireworks is not likely to garner his attention. As he pulls into the driveway of his new friend's home, he fails to see the familiar silver Lincoln creeping up behind him. I observe. I watch my son dismount and discard his bike on the soft wet grass. I see him walk to the door and ring the bell. Another boy answers. He looks older than Gabriel. They talk for a minute or two and then the older looking boy goes back in to the house. Gabriel goes back to his bike, lifts it up and sits on the seat, wet from the

20

grass. His face is expressionless. He walks his bike to the curb and sits beneath a street lamp where, for the first time, he sees me sitting in the car. He doesn't move or change the expression on his face.

I get out of the car and walk up to my son. "What's going on," I say. "Nothing," replies Gabriel, momentarily drained of his emotions. He is sweating and wet from the fog and his brilliant black eyes have lost their luster.

"How 'bout we get something to eat. Wanna go to Taco Bell?" I ask.

"No," he says, confused and embarrassed and desperately trying to preserve his machismo.

"Come on," I cajole him, "I know you must be hungry."

"No," he says again.

"So what are you going to do?" I ask him.

"Stay here," says Gabriel.

"Where? You're sleeping on the street. That's your plan?" I say. "Come on. Come home. Throw your bike in the trunk and let's get out of here."

"I'm staying here," he restates emphatically.

"Okay," I say. "Then so am I."

"No!" screams Gabriel. "Go home!"

"You know I can't do that."

"I hate you," says Gabriel, as if it's a conditioned reflex—and he stands—and he grabs his bike—and he walks over to the car and places it in the trunk—and then he kicks the side of the car as if he's testing its tires, leaving a black mark on the fender from the sole of his sneakers.

I say nothing. *I hate you* is pretty mild in the general development of Gabriel's recent acquisition of new language. I hear it so often that it has no bite. He will learn new phrases, new ways to cause me pain if I let him. One day he will say, *you're not my real father.* He will say it to hurt me, but when the words come out of his mouth for the first time, they will lack the poison of his conviction, diminished by years of verbal abuse directed at Paula and me. When he says it, I will feel nothing. My body and mind will be numb to the horror

21

that his mouth will someday be.

In the car the leather seats are cold. We're not talking. Gabriel is exhausted and I am simply drained. "Take me to Taco Bell," he demands.

"Okay," I answer.

It's nearly midnight when we get home. Gabriel takes his tacos and soda and nachos down to the basement where he will surely fall asleep watching television. I smile at Paula. "Another happy ending," I say. "But Paula, he crossed Ryder's Lane," and we both know what that means. Ryder's Lane is a very busy road and a very real boundary for Gabriel's travels on two wheels. It is an invisible fence distinguished by cars moving at fifty miles an hour or more. If the fence no longer exists, then we can no longer control Gabriel's whereabouts. It's like he's learned to ride a bike all over again, except now he is eleven not seven. At seven you go round and round the block. The exhilaration of speed and freedom runs parallel to childish innocence and therefore keeps you home and safe. At seven a bike is fun and wonderful, it's not yet perceived as a serious mode of transportation. At nearly twelve, however, when traffic and fog and cars and night no longer create apprehensions, a young boy's universe is opened in fantastic and troublesome ways.

●

I love this boy and I write about this boy. And it is eight years since he rode his bike through the invisible fence. And so much has happened and he has hurt so many people in so many ways. Yet still I have a compassion, a love, a misery that I call my life. It frightens me when I think about it…this life of mine with Gabriel. How does it end? When does the man I want him to be blossom from his desperate and awful innocence? He sees my passion for him and he works it to his advantage. He breaks me down. Like a virus once eradicated, he returns with newer and deadlier threats. And what do I do? I keep on writing. It's all I have. But the writing has changed. I have changed. My passion is different. My passion is to tell this story now, not so much through my formerly sympathetic eye, but through a heart that is wounded and may never fully beat as it once had. It's my story now, mine and Gabriel's. And in the end, if it ever ends, I may come to understand the subtleties of love that currently elude me.

.

Chapter 3

"Take a look," said the doctor, leading me to the black microscope on the stainless steel counter. "This is your sperm. I took it from the semen sample you gave me when you arrived. We'll do a complete semen analysis over the next few days, but I can tell you right now that you have an issue with motility and morphology." Motility: those are the poor swimmers. Morphology: those are the sperm without tails.

So I looked through the microscope and sure enough a gathering of my sperm was swimming in circles and a whole lot more weren't swimming at all. Paula stood beside me. She wore a short red skirt and a blue and white blouse that clung to her as if she had just come in from the rain. She looked good. No, she looked great. When I lifted my head from the microscope to meet her glance, she smiled and said, "What does it look like."

"It looks like they're waiting for a bus," I said, not at all happy about the things I was seeing with one eye shut.

For ten years I had known that I might have a problem. It's called a varicocele and during a routine college physical, the doctor pointed out a cluster of veins on one side of my scrotum. "You might have problems when you're older," he said. "It's just something you should know now."

So when Paula got pregnant the first time, I postulated that the problem wasn't so severe. Stupid doctors, what do they know? My sperm was kicking ass. But I was wrong. After six months of trying to get pregnant again, and obviously no luck, I was advised to seek the assistance of a male infertility specialist.

"It looks like you have a varicocele problem," he said, juggling my testicles between the latex gloved fingers of his right hand. *Got that right*, I thought, as I let go of the tiny vestige of hope that I was not the problem.

To be fair, he was gentle. He handled my testicles in a delicate manner, like he was separating the yolk from the egg white: back and forth, up and down, carefully shifting my manhood between his thumb and forefinger.

When he was through he said, "There are lots of veins surrounding your testicles. These veins are bringing too much blood to the area, which makes it very warm down there. There are also valves in your arteries that control the flow of blood, but it appears that your valves are not functioning properly. If they were working properly, the valves would close every time you stood up, restricting the blood flow—essentially keeping things down there cool. When they malfunction, as yours do, too much blood surrounds the testicles. That creates more heat than is necessary. Too much heat kills sperm, or in your case, affects their shape. It's really remarkable that your wife got pregnant at all, but it's no surprise that it hasn't happened again."

"So what we do," he went on to say, "is cut the main artery and tie it off, restricting the flow of blood. Over time, the area cools down, and sperm production becomes normal. In your case, it looks like both sides have valves that don't work, so we'll do a double varicocele operation."

None of this was good, but fortunately for us there was still lots of time to create a family. Another setback? Yes, but not insurmountable. Paula was pregnant once, she'll be pregnant again, and next time the pregnancy will joyfully end with a healthy son or a daughter.

We were young and improbably confident about things for which we had no control. It's an illusion of the mind. We think that the world is balanced: everyone is having babies, we will have babies too. The simple fact that my sperm count was low and that the sperm I was producing lacked the ability to swim through the vast interior forest of the female anatomy mattered not a lick. Without any rational reason to believe we would win this battle, we simply believed that we would. All sadness aside, we continued to be optimistic.

The irony, of course, is that now Paula and I would have identical scars across our lower abdomens. Couples, especially married couples, share everything. So why shouldn't Paula and I share a scar? Her ectopic. My double varicocele.

Eight months earlier, on a cool March morning, Paula emerged from the bathroom with a short white stick in her hand. She handed it to me and said "Does that look blue to you?" referring to the barely visible line of blue at the end of the stick that looked like a cotton swab without the cotton.

I examined it carefully, knowing full well the implications of answering yes. "It's very faint," I said. "Are you pregnant?" She smiled and I said, "Really?"

"I don't know," said Paula with a slightly dazed, slightly thrilled look on her face. "It's not like my periods have ever been regular. But I feel a little different... so maybe."

And so began Paula's first pregnancy, fraught with uncertainty, filled with hope, joyful and worrisome for all the right reasons.

It's a funny thing when you're pregnant for the first time. We weren't trying, but we weren't not trying either. And then, presto, the stick is blue. We were two young adults without a care in the world, moving through life with a self-assurance that we would be okay. It wasn't long, however, before the naïve simplicity of our notions came crashing down with Paula's first pregnancy.

So the line was blue, barely blue. Would it have mattered if it were a rich shade of navy, a glistening saphire? Perhaps in my mind it would have, although I learned rather quickly that a woman can't be a little pregnant. It's everything or nothing, there's no in between. So we were blissfully ecstatic when the everything was confirmed by the doctor. It was our time to create miniature versions of ourselves. It was our time to enter the world of parenting. And it was my turn to not repeat the mistakes of my mother and father. (It's what all parents hope for, right...to be better than those who walked before us.) That's what I hoped for; that's what I dreamed. My sons and daughters would talk to me, they would seek my advice, and they would want to spend time together. There was nothing novel to the plan. But first they had to be born.

●

On the morning of my surgery, a nurse came into my room and shaved me. I thought she would just shave the area of the incision, but evidently there are pesky germs ruminating throughout the entire pubic region and so she took it upon herself to remove every vestige of post pubescent growth. She was an ordinary looking woman, although I was instantly reminded of a stripper I once saw at a Saints and Sinners picnic who wore a nurse's uniform and carried a six-foot long hypodermic needle. I was seventeen and my father brought me to the picnic. He said it would be fun, and it was.

Next came the valium and before I knew it I was lying on my back in the operating room. There were people and lights and machines and nurses with regular length hypodermics, all talking and milling about. Thank God for the valium that kept me calm. I waited for what seemed forever before I got my instructions from the anesthesiologist. He said, "Would you please begin to count backwards from one hundred?"

I said, "One hundred. Ninety-nine. Ninety-eight."

When I woke up there were fifteen or so staples holding together that very smooth region four inches below my belly button. In a week, the staples would come out. In three months, the thirty to forty million sperm that my body created for regular inseminations of Paula, would be doing the back stroke through her vagina looking for that very magical egg.

"You're fine," said the doctor. "The morphology and motility are very good." And once again he led me to the black microscope on the stainless steel counter where this time I watch my sperm go up and down and right and left. No little doggies going in circles. Every sperm had a long tail that whipped back and forth, reminding me of the tadpoles I caught when I was a boy. And although there was no place for them to go, squeezed between two thin pieces of glass, there would be many future, long-distance opportunities for my little swimmers to reach their ultimate destination.

●

Within twenty-four hours of telling just about everyone on the planet that she was pregnant, Paula began to cramp and spot blood. I knew zilch, of course, and confidently said, "It's nothing, don't worry." Even the doctor suggested it was too soon to worry. Another day went by and the spotting stopped. And another day went by and the spotting and cramps resumed. Now we were nervous. This could mean three things: It could be the first signs of a miscarriage. It could be an ectopic pregnancy in which the pregnancy is stuck in one of the fallopian tubes. Or hopefully, wonderfully and happily, it could mean absolutely nothing.

On the fourth day, Paula was still spotting and was not feeling well at all. We went to the doctor's office where her OB/GYN examined her. He removed a gloved hand from her body and I could see that it was covered in blood. It startled me but evidently there was not enough blood to warrant any more than a wait-and-see response so early in the pregnancy.

On the fifth day, the cramping intensified and at the doctor's instruction, Paula went immediately to the hospital. It was there that we were told that they would have to do exploratory surgery to determine if the pregnancy was ectopic. If it was, then the doctor would do his best to remove the pregnancy and save Paula's fallopian tube. Either way, it looked like this pregnancy was over.

On the outside, Paula appeared strong even though we both knew that the best case scenario was pretty awful. I held her hand. I told her I loved her. I looked at her fear and tried to cover my own, assuring her that everything would be fine. There was still a very slim chance that this could be something minor, something fixable. All that faith in our invincibility had to be worth something. So we held on to that hope, as if not doing so would crush every dream we ever had.

It's fair to say that this was the beginning of our sadness, a sadness that would rise and fall like a chair on a Ferris wheel that never stops, never fully fades away into the distant horizon. It was also the beginning of our lives in an altered universe—the universe of the infertile—the universe of adoption—and ultimately the universe of fear. All of this for two people with the smallest of aspirations, to be no different than any other family in the world.

The doctors were able to save the fallopian tube. They removed the pregnancy and told us that Paula should have little trouble conceiving again, although there would be a greater risk for another ectopic pregnancy. In our minds, however, this was a one-time nightmare not to be repeated in our lifetime. We could still hold on to our dreams of little people who looked and talked and acted like us, and embodied all the best that we had to offer the world. That's what I told my parents through the tears—we could still have children; Paula would be fine; the swimmers would swim again. That's what I told everyone and everyone believed me.

Chapter 4

There are bad things afoot, things you should know. There are horrible things that I will do and Gabriel has done, and somewhere in the blurry picture of my thoughts there is the buried memory of an absolute and pure love. That's the best I can do; so I hold on to that memory. I can tell you that I love my son and that all I ever wanted was what was best for him. I can say that I did everything that I could do, everything I could afford. But none of it—still—ever—was enough. Was I right? Was I wrong? The goodness that I hoped for and the direction that I sought for Gabriel's life have never fully materialized. In nearly every instance of choice, when Gabriel could pick between the light from the dark, he invariably chose the dark. And what could I do short of chains and shackles and medication and counseling and all this wasted love? Save him from himself? I had faith, so much faith, but it has lapsed. I had a wonderful, beautiful passion for my endless love. I had Gabriel. He was mine.

●

Every door to my home is closed. This is not a metaphor, this is a story. The doors are closed, but I know that Gabriel is home. He closes the doors to detect my arrival. I could enter through the garage door, let it open slowly, screeching along its metal tracks, announcing to the entire block that I have arrived, or I could go to the back door, and if Gabriel has not checked it, I can simply walk in unannounced. Or I can try the front door, but usually it's locked and I would certainly be heard. So I go to the back. I look through the slits of the blue plastic vertical blinds and see Gabriel sitting at the family computer. I can only imagine what he is doing. My ten-year-old boy has already been accused of cyber-terrorism. "The next time I see you, I'm gonna take a knife to your gut." That's what he said to a boy who was moving in on his ten-year-old girlfriend. It took a very long and painful conversation to avert a legal nightmare. When the dust settled and once again Gabriel was allowed to troll the unholy universe of the World Wide Web, I discovered that he had opened his mind to an unfettered galaxy of Internet stimulation. So I slide the door open and walk in. Gabriel turns from the desk and looks at me. I look back at him and the computer and the printer. A picture begins to emerge of a smiling young girl, her breasts are large and inviting, her nipples dark and pointed as if someone had placed an ice cube on them before taking the picture. And in case you were concerned, there was not a hint of clothing to be found on her perfect Barbie doll body.

Gabriel is nonplussed. After all, what's a naked girl compared to his murderous thoughts? He says, "Ya caught me," smiles, stands, and walks away, as the printer completes the ankles and toes and slowly expels Barbie resting beneath a striped beach umbrella. In the incredible perversity of my world, this father and son moment seems almost innocent. Little Gabriel, becoming a man, looking at porn—isn't that sweet?

So I take a deep breath. I'm reminded of the stacks of Playboy magazines my father kept in his closet behind a few shoe boxes. And, of course, the really nasty stuff in his sock drawer. It's only sex, right? What's a little porn between a boy and a computer? It's better this than guns, which seems to be his other preoccupation. Gabriel is totally and utterly obsessed with them. Everything becomes a weapon. But he is also obsessed with Pokémon cards. The darkness and the light are a constant shadow upon him, and my only hope is that when he chooses, he chooses correctly.

A few weeks later he goes to Florida to visit his grandparents, Paula's mother and father. He travels alone and I admire his bravery in doing so. I also admire and really like this other side of my son— the piece of him that connects him to family—my parents, Paula's parents, all his cousins and aunts and uncles. He adores them all, and they adore him. They love him and want to be with him. At his best he is still precocious and engaging. He hugs me and tells me he loves me when he boards the plane. And when he returns nearly a week later, he runs to my open arms.

In Florida, Gabriel can ride his skateboard anywhere in the expansive retirement community and not worry about getting hit by a speeding car. The speed limit is 15 miles an hour and most of the residents travel slower than that. He can swim in the big heated swimming pool, watch as much television as he wants, and even go on the Internet, all under the watchful and devoted eyes of his grandmother and grandfather.

And he can go to the mall, which is a little bit like heaven since he knows he will never leave empty handed. He is, after all, the grandson. So an excursion to the mall is a nearly daily activity during his five day sojourn in Florida.

Gabriel and his grandmother are walking in the Boynton Beach Mall. It's not a very big mall but does have two large anchor stores at either end. By comparison, the Boynton Beach Mall is diminutive when placed against the monolithic and up-scale Mall at Boca Raton, just fifteen minutes away. Nonetheless, it serves its purpose for a grandmother and her grandson. They are on their way to a clothing store that sells predominately black t-shirts, assorted chains, wrist bands and temporary tattoos that resemble dragons and skulls. Suddenly, and with not a hint of elaboration or noise, Paula's mother is pushed to the ground and relieved of her purse. Gabriel, for the first time in his brief life, recognizes that something bad has taken place in front of his eyes, although it is uncertain if in his mind the bad thing was stealing the purse or knocking over his grandmother. No matter. He quickly pulls his grandmother up to her feet, assesses the damage, (she is fine) and takes off after the thief. My ten-year-old son is racing after a man that I later learned to be twenty-something years old, a convicted criminal and well over 200 pounds. I can only imagine the scene as my ninety-pound mop head boy races after an overweight thug clutching a black and red leather purse. "Stop," screams Gabriel, as he races past the Victoria's Secret. "Get the Police," he shouts as he the dashes through the food court, chasing the thief into the parking lot. "You won't get away," he huffs in his sweet ten-year-old voice, as two armed security guards, waiting at the exit ramp, pounce on the thief.

The next day it's all over the news...well, at least, in Boynton Beach, Florida: Grandson Chases Mugger. And the parents...we are shocked, thrilled, proud, overjoyed and only mildly concerned that this episode might not have ended so happily. In the instant where light and dark clashed, the light shone brilliantly on Gabriel. He had done what was not only right, but was also brave and noble. Despite the cyber-threat a few months before, we still believed that he had a chance, this random act of kindness being more than enough to give us hope.

I believed in God, in love, and in the goodness within all of us. I believed in the supernatural strength of my own ability to influence and control and make whole this thing that was so much more than a lump of clay to shape. So when he screamed at me, I said to myself that at least he's not afraid of me, and no child should fear his father. And when stuff began to disappear from the house, I told myself that I was getting careless and forgetful. And he still liked to hang out with me a bit, and I thought that that was cool too. But I could also see that life was getting the better of him until finally he ceased to be my hero or anti-hero; he was just a burden I couldn't fix. And then I thought I did (fix him) but I really didn't until worse became a nightmare and hell became damnation and everything good and kind and wonderful in my life was tainted by the stain of my out-of-control son.

Chapter 5

My car is new. It's the color of the sky and shines like glitter and smells like vinyl and reminds me that I am not too old to be impractical. Late at night when I am sure not to hit a kid on his bike or an elderly woman walking to the curb to retrieve her mail, I take my car, my new car, my three hundred and forty horsepower two-door thrill, and obliterate the speed limits on the winding country roads through the few remaining farms of central New Jersey.

Gabriel thinks my car is hot. He shows it off to his friends and has me take his picture standing beside it, looking like he owns it, looking like a cool kid with a really cool car. He tells his friends that in four years, when he is twenty-one, that I will give the car to him. His friends are impressed. He is impressed. I am doubtful.

I am doubtful because I know a secret. I know that there is a symbiotic relationship between a man and his machine, especially if that machine is a car. I know that this car will not like Gabriel because Gabriel has not been nice to it, has not been nice to me. There are two small, barely noticeable, indentations from his knuckles on the passenger side door, where Gabriel punched the car in anger. There is a scratch on the hood from the time he tossed a trash can lid at me as I backed out of the driveway. And there is a broken vanity mirror on the flip side of the front passenger seat visor. Paula pulls it down to look at herself as she applies burgundy red lipstick to her mouth. What she sees are four diagonal cracks from the bottom of the mirror to its top. The cracks come together to form a perfect isosceles triangle that cuts from below her chin to the top of her nose. Although mathematically perfect in its dimensions, it is a familiar reminder of how imperfect Gabriel can be. His imperfections are often revealed by the swiftness of his fists.

Dents. Holes. Broken glass. Broken hearts.

I'm looking at that picture of him standing beside the car. He swaggers. He thinks that the car is a chick magnet, and maybe it is. It's certainly an improvement on the last family vehicle. But this car is not meant for families; it's meant for fun. Still, as I look at the picture, I am reminded of another incident with another car when Gabriel was not even fourteen years old. It was a time in Gabriel's life when he was a hider; he hid all sorts of things. But I am a finder, I find everything. I'd go through his stuff and occasionally discover new hiding places for the crap he didn't want me to know about. To be honest, he was not very clever at the art of hiding, and most of the objects he didn't want me to find were easily found. His favorite hiding place was under his mattress, but he also hid things in his pillows, his clothing, his nightstand, his guitar case, his dresser and occasionally in the stuffing of the carnival animals that I won for him at the County Fair. The most common finds are cigarette lighters: right there—one at a time—under his mattress. I knew I couldn't control his smoking but I was concerned that an accidental act of friction might set his bed on fire. So I took the lighters and kept them in a collection at my office. I also knew that he was stealing the lighters since he had no money. These were not the cheap plastic lighters one purchased at the Seven-Eleven, but rather the fancy stainless steel lighters with etchings of skulls or marijuana leaves or a fish simulating oral sex. He stole them from the stores at the mall; I stole them from him.

I find other things too. I find knives, razors, and candy bars and cookies that he hoards like a child who has never tasted chocolate. I find porn...hard...soft...whatever. Once I opened his nightstand drawer and I found a gun. When I saw it, I became nauseous. I picked it up and it was heavy; it had the weight of an instrument of death. Upon closer examination I could see that it was not a real gun at all, but a BB gun designed to look like a German luger, or at least what I thought a German luger might look like. To identify itself as a non-lethal weapon there was a small plastic orange circle at the tip of the gun, at that spot where the BB is expelled through an equally small hole. So I took the gun into the garage, found a hammer, and smashed it into a hundred little pieces of broken plastic and bent metal.

Mostly, Gabriel said nothing when I removed the things that he knew he should not have. After all, anything stolen could always be replaced. And I told him about the gun. And I told him how it freaked me out. And he told me it belonged to a friend. And I told him tough shit.

One day, during my usual rounds of investigation, I found two unopened packs of cigarettes. They were hardly hidden at all, caught between the frame of his bed and his mattress. As I took them out of the bed frame I pressed the small white and green boxes against my lips. I inhaled. I smelled the tobacco through the cellophane wrap that crinkled each time I squeezed them lightly in my palm. I could see him with his smokes; he was easy to visualize: a changeling with an attitude. He grows a few inches, he gains a few pounds, he plops a cigarette in his mouth.

He was sitting on the corner by the fire hydrant in a sleeveless white t-shirt. His arms are far from developed, and his hands and wrists are covered with black and red ink, a reflection of boredom and opposition, and another stay-out-of-my-face day at school. There was a long line of drawings and crosses and names and pentagrams and swirly figures that extended from the top of his hands to his biceps. They came together in a bodily rendering of early adolescent imagination. He had made himself the temporarily tattooed man, the boy-man with a cigarette dangling from his lips, like he was some kind of James Dean, although for sure he could never tell you who James Dean was.

He flies into the house around six in the evening. On this particular day, he skipped the school bus and walked straight to a friend's house to do whatever he does with his friends—nothing truly bad as far as I knew. All the truly bad stuff was reserved for the house. For me. For Paula. For frightening his brothers.

Paula was at work. I was home. Ethan watched TV. Jonathan occupied himself with a Lego project.

Gabriel was the King of Lego. By the time he was three years old he was putting together complicated Lego animals and cars and machines that were meant to be assembled by children much older than he. He could spend hours working on his Legos and we gladly bought him expensive and more sophisticated designs. It seemed to be a wonderful use of his hands, mind and imagination. It was great to watch a child work in three dimensions, and to be able to imagine a three dimensional future for that child.

Soon Gabriel discovered that his cigarettes were missing. He knew who took them too. Without an ounce of fear he said to me, "Gimme my cigarettes. I know you took them. They're mine. I want them back."

"I don't want you smoking," I said.

"Give them to me," he repeated.

"No," I said, and walked away.

He followed me. "They're my Goddamn cigarettes. I want them. You can't take them. They are not yours!"

I repeated, "I don't like you smoking."

I walked into my bedroom and he followed me. "What the fuck is wrong with you," he said. "Gimme my Goddamn cigarettes," and then he kicked my bedroom door and spit on the floor.

I was calm. I was always calm. It was disturbing how calm I was, as I said with an air of indifference. "What makes you think I have them?"

"I know you go through my shit. They're my fucking cigarettes," he screamed.

I left the bedroom and went back to the kitchen.

"Dad's being an ass-hole," he yelled for his brothers to hear, and then he shouted again, "I want my fucking cigarettes. Why can't you just give me my fucking cigarettes?"

Ethan and Jonathan were nervous. I knew the look and it was painful to watch.

Jonathan said, "Are the police going to come?"

"No," I said. "Not today."

"Dad," said Ethan. "Just give 'em to him."

"I can't," I told him.

"Give them to me," screamed Gabriel. "Why are you being such a fucking pussy?"

"Stop it, Gabriel," I said. And I took Ethan and Jonathan by their hands and walked them to their room. Gabriel followed us.

"You know I won't stop," he said. "You know I won't. I want my fucking cigarettes."

Ethan repeats his plea, "Dad, just give him the cigarettes."

I wanted to feel bad for Ethan and Jonathan. I wanted to explain to them what happened to our lives, why our family is different from everyone else's. But all I could do is protect them for the moment as I drew the enemy out.

"Stay in your room," I said to the boys as I closed the door behind them.

Gabriel didn't care about them; he only cared about me. I left the boys in their room, turned, and walked past Gabriel's bedroom door.

"Fuck," he screamed.

He was right behind me. I heard him puffing. I felt his anger. I didn't have to see his face to feel the intensity of his glare. He passed his room on the right and he kicked the door with the full force of his soon-to-be fourteen-year-old body. I heard it crack but didn't turn to see if there was any damage. At least this time it didn't come off its hinges.

We're back in the kitchen. "What the fuck is wrong with you?" he shouted.

I was doing my best to stay within myself, yet I couldn't help but wonder what I had wrought. What kind of child is this? What kind of human being? What kind of father had I become that I had allowed my life and my son to reach this horrible point in time?

Gabriel opened the silverware drawer and removed a large carving knife. The grip is as long as my hand and the blade is double the length of the grip. "Put the knife down," I said.

"Gimme my cigarettes."

"Put the knife down."

"Gimme my cigarettes."

"Put it down,"

"Give 'em to me."

I paused. My son was threatening me with a knife for five dollars worth of cigarettes. What is this insanity that is my life? Thank God Paula wasn't there. I should have called the Police, of course…I should have. Isn't that what his shrink said? He said he was worried that someday Gabriel might hurt us. I said I don't believe that. But he was holding a knife. At me. In my house.

I left the house and began walking. "You fucking pussy," he screamed at me. "Where the fuck are you going?"

I said nothing. I was walking, walking away. I was leaving my children alone with a lunatic. But they were safe; he would never hurt them. Only me. Only me. Only for me and Paula did he save these special moments of madness. He was not even fourteen and we had endured years of verbal and sometimes physical abuse. Were we victims? Yes. Were we enablers? Yes. Did we have any control at all? Not really. Not any more. But maybe it was me. What was I doing taking him on, challenging him? Was I trying to be a good parent? I was no parent to this child, to my son, to my beloved.

Suddenly, I was pushed. He was one hundred and twenty pounds to my two hundred and five, and he threw himself at me. Two small but powerful hands were thrust into my back, just below my shoulder blades. I lurched forward, catching myself in mid fall, and continued to walk.

"Gimme my fucking cigarettes," I heard yet again.

"Stop it," I said. "I am going for a walk."

And I turn and look and see that in his hand he was no longer holding the carving knife. He was holding my Ping five iron and swinging it around as if he was trying to protect himself from being attacked by invisible demons.

I approached him slowly…intently. I was three feet away. Two. One. I spoke calmly but with force. I said, "Gabriel, go for it. Take one swing, that's all it takes. You want out of this family? You will never come back. They will take you away and you will never see us again. I'm begging you. Please. Hit me. I won't hit back. Put me out of my fucking misery you fucking pussy."

"Just gimme my Goddamn cigarettes," he pleaded. "They're not yours; they're mine."

I wanted to teach him to play golf. It's something fathers and sons do. Keep your head down. Relax your grip. Nice and easy now. You're one hundred and sixty five yards from the green... perfect for a five iron. Remember, you don't have to kill the ball.

And then, of course, I saw the truth. It's not over yet but I had clearly lost. I always lost when I sank to his level. I tried not to go there, but I would be lying if I said it didn't happen often. He was a master at sucking me in, at drawing me down, at bringing out my most base instincts.

With my club in his hand, he ran back to the house, leaving me standing on the sidewalk. His brothers were waiting for us. I could see them in the garage, holding their respective yellow and red bicycles, using them as a shield between themselves and Gabriel. They were watching the end-game. I was watching too as Gabriel made his last play. He stood beside my car in the driveway. He held the club above the windshield and screamed one last time, "I—want—my—fucking—cigarettes!"

How was it that no one had seen or heard us? How was it that not one of my neighbors, one who knew our situation (they all knew our situation) had not yet called the police? Where were the neighbors? Where were the police?

I said nothing as I walked back to the house. I looked at Ethan and Jonathan and I was horrified and angry with myself for exposing them yet again to Gabriel's anger.

"What are you going to do?" asked Jonathan.

"It's okay," I told him as I walked past him and into the house. "Wait right here. Everything is okay."

Once inside the house, I went to my bedroom and found my own secret hiding place. I opened the closet and shoved all of the clothes on the clothes bar—my suits, shirts, pants, ties, belts and jackets— to one side, revealing a charcoal gray, double-breasted pin-striped suit, 42 regular, that hung alone against the closet wall. It was my wedding suit from eighteen years and twenty pounds ago. I reached inside the right breast pocket and as I did I could hear the crinkle of cellophane and smell the slight odor of tobacco.

I squeezed the boxes tightly, hoping to crush a few cigarettes in the process. I was out of my mind, but I also knew that it had to stop, and this (I hate myself for admitting it) was the only way to make it (him) stop.

Gabriel was standing by the car, club in hand, joking with his brothers. It was amazing how quickly he could transform himself from beast to buddy, but I had seen it so many times before. Yet he is not a schizophrenic and he does not have multiple personalities. He was a loon, plain and simple. Sociopathic? Probably. Maybe. But still a loon.

"Gabriel," I said, gaining his attention, watching his immediate transformation back to the nightmare that he had been for the last twenty minutes.

"What," he replied with absolute disdain.

"Go fuck yourself."

And I took the cigarettes and hurled them into the street where they mingled with a flattened can of Pepsi, a brown torn wrapper from a Hershey Bar and the remnants of my masculinity.

Chapter 6

Iwas born on Long Island, New York, but grew up in New Jersey and went to college in Ohio. I have worked for the Boy Scouts of America, a community college, a medical school and two universities. My eyes are green, my hair is gray and my waist is four inches larger than it should be for a man who exercises as much as I do. I live a stone's throw from the New Jersey Turnpike.

I love my son, (I love all of my sons) yet my heart has been shattered often by him and the things I have had to do. I had this incredible, wonderful, beautiful, charismatic and smart son that was pissing his life away. By the time he was fourteen, I had lost control of him. So I sent him away to the woods and to boarding school. And for fifteen months he sat in a classroom in Georgia where he might learn to control his anger and possibly understand that there are better ways to negotiate than throwing a baseball bat through a window.

Occasionally, he would write. Here is a letter he sent me two weeks after he arrived at his North Carolina therapeutic wilderness program.

> *Dear Dad,*
>   *I hate your fucking guts and when I get home I am going to kill you. Then I am going to burn down your house, you fucking piece of shit. How are my brothers? Tell them I miss them.*
>   *Love,*
>   *Gabe*

That pretty much covers Gabriel. My life is a dichotomy of

love and hate but Gabriel is a violent attention deficit disordered hyperactively defiant bipolar enigma.

I also have a wife, who, of course is this story's heroine. Gabriel is the protagonist and I am the Devil. Yes, the Devil. Just ask my son, Ethan, who, as I am trying to get him to do his homework, often refers to me as Satan-like in nature, if not spirit. Ironically, that makes him the Devil's spawn, a characterization that hardly brings him pleasure.

So I see that Ethan is struggling with his homework and I say in my best Darth Vader voice, "Ethan, you are the Devil's spawn."

"Nooooooo," he screams, and he runs out the door, his arms flailing as if a swarm of bees were attacking him.

"Get back here," I yell, but it is too late, the Devil has planted his seed.

No matter. I have come to accept the fact that I am not a good person for reasons far beyond the well-intentioned teasing that expresses itself to be the mental torture of my sons. My wife, on the other hand, has done nothing to deserve to live in the dysfunctionality of our family unit. When I met her she was a graduate student at Ohio University studying to become a clinical psychologist. I was a career man with the Boy Scouts of America, having graduated from OU a year earlier. We were two northeastern Jews stuck in the southern part of a northern industrial state with a clearly southern bent to its way of life.

That was twenty-seven years ago, around the time I ran my last marathon. Since then, we adopted one son who would very much like to return us to the earth from which all things are born, gave birth to a second son, who is as sweet as hyacinth but struggles with the nuances of life, and also gave birth to a third son who, despite the extreme and often dysfunctional nature of our family unit, is an intriguing replication of our best parts.

Paula is an extraordinary and brave woman; she is also having an affair. Consequently, our sex life has never—and I do mean never never never—been better better better. Okay, I'm lying (at least I think I'm lying). Not about the sex, the sex has been phenomenal and often. In fact, were it not for my belief that no child should ever read about their parents' sexual proclivities, (Don't we screw our kids up enough?) I would be happy to share some, if not all of the lovely details.

Now, here is the thing about the affair that is most interesting. Besides the obvious sexual benefits to me, (Is it her guilt or a new awakening, and should I even care?) it's not really an affair in the classic sense. If it were, why would Paula bother having sex with me at all? Her lover, whom I shall call Andre, (his real name is Anthony) would be banging her brains out on a regular basis, and I would be renewing my relationship with my dear friend Rosie Palm. She would be worn out and I would be a little gimpy. Neither is the case because this is a deep and thoughtful and absolutely cerebral Internet affair, for which I am not sure there exists a contemporary definition beyond what I have just described.

Paula and Andre were high-school sweethearts. Like millions of others across the globe, they reconnected in 21st century cyber-space. I believe he was her first. From what I knew, there seemed to be a good deal of adolescent passion between Paula and Andre. Yet college and marriage and children and distance and time were more than enough to squelch two kids who were nuts about each other. Life went on. Still, after twenty-two years of me, Paula not so secretly sought him out and found him, reminding me that each of us yearns to find a place in the past that's always better than the present.

Here's a little perspective: Andre did the west coast Ivy League thing. By the time he was thirty his fortune was growing exponentially. His cliff-side house on the Pacific Ocean was an architectural marvel that he shared with his wife and three dogs. His stunning wife was a cross between Catherine Deneuve and Meryl Streep with one exception: they were normal, she was nuts.

Andre wants to leave his wife. He is buying her a million-dollar house of her own to ease her pain (or his guilt) when he officially throws her out. Andre is in a lot of pain. Paula is in a lot of pain. I'm in a lot of pain. I could be wrong, but it wouldn't surprise me if there was a third house in the offing for the little gal whose sexual appetite I now blissfully enjoy. I am thinking—no, hoping, that if the cyber affair ends badly that maybe Andre will want to date me. I may be a little too old to take up the down low. But what-the-hell! I can be taught.

Yet the girl went home with me forever…me, with my career with the Boy Scouts of America, my hiking boots and my chainsaw…me, who in 1983 decided that I would make my fortune as a professional fundraiser…me, who never had a house remotely close to a body of water…me, who yearned for something else but was lucky enough to marry a very brave women. Rick and Paula: two unexceptionally normal parents surviving their lunatic son.

Along the way, I began to write. I wrote about my wedding day: *It was lovely and the bride was beautiful. The sun shone down on Paula and me and our hearts were warm and full and ready to begin a wonderful journey through life together.* I wrote about Gabriel and the incredible void his birth filled in our lives: *How had we ever lived without a child to bless us?* And I wrote about him again when he was expelled for the first time: *Couldn't the principal see how wrong this was!* And I wrote about him again as he became increasingly violent: *I never heard an eleven year old curse like that before.* And I wrote about him again when we sent him away: *Not a word was uttered; he simply left with the escorts.* And when he came back. And when he went to the mental hospital. And when he went to jail. And when he went to court. And finally… suddenly… amazingly, I saw what I instinctively knew all along but could never admit… there would be no happy ending because I was hopeless and the life had been sucked out of me, turning all my plums into prunes.

Where was the hope? Where was the salvation? Where was the epiphany? And I said there is no hope! There is no salvation! There is no epiphany! There was me and Gabriel and our ability (if we were lucky) to survive each other.

●

A couple years ago I was being interviewed for a really big job. I didn't need the job, but I was always eager to make more money and I knew that minimally my resumé was strong enough to get me in the door. As interviews went, it wasn't the worst interview of my life. The worst interview of my life was when I was trying to become the head of athletic fundraising for a major New Jersey university. I told the Athletic Director, a crusty old man with a neck the size of Idaho, that if any of my sons ever decided to play football that I would personally break their legs before they had a chance to set foot on the field. I think that if he could have jumped across the table and ripped out my tonsils, he would have. I witnessed a slow blaze that moved north from his neck to his temples. By the time the interview was over, his face resembled a scarlet sunset and my career in university athletics was over.

But that's the thing about interviews. Sometimes you just say what you feel. Ordinarily, that makes sense. As for me, I am a firm believer in honesty, especially when it involves the truth.

So the head-hunter for the really big job said to me, "Tell me about the life defining moments in your life?"

Huh? I wondered inside my head, scrambling for a deep and profound thought. Life defining moments! What the hell does that mean? What does a fricking life defining moment have to do with my ability to raise money? I can do this job and you can pay me a lot more money than I'm making now. Trick question. This isn't fair.

So I did what I do best when placed in an uncomfortable situation. I began to sweat. Not a lot, but enough to force me to swipe my brow with my hand on more than one occasion.

"You know," I said, as teeny weenie drops of sweat gathered in the wrinkles in my brow, "It's not really something I ever thought about."

And that was it. I could see the look on her face. *This man is not a deep thinker; he is not the man for us.*

Since then, I think about this question a lot. What has defined me? What has made me successful? What has made me cynical?

What has made me friendless? I am a father, a writer, a leader, a husband, a brother, a son, a subordinate, an artist, and an athlete. Like most people, however, the perception of my defining characteristics runs parallel to my profession. I am a fundraiser, and a damn good one. But I am also just another person who manages to get through the day by fooling those around him with an aura of confidence. I stink of confidence and I control it like a chef who never measures his spices but always uses just the right amount. How did this happen?

I have memories. Swimming with my mother in the lake—falling off my bike—being hit by my parents—winning at wrestling—the first time I got laid—the first time I made love—the first time I got drunk—the first time I got high—my wedding—Gabriel's birth—Ethan's birth—Jonathan's birth—Paula's many lost pregnancies—the day I bought my first car—the day I got my first job—the day I got the job I really wanted twenty years later—the night we sent Gabriel away—the crying—the crying—the crying.

I am jaded and I am lost and trying to write a beautiful and loving tale about a boy whose soul is intimately intertwined with my own. It is Gabriel and me and Paula and the boys and the truth and the lies and the mystery and the love. Is there hope? I don't know. Mountains of sadness and sorrow continue to thrust their bitter peaks toward the sky, converting me to a cynic in a world unable to comprehend the perversity of my circumstances. Too often, life simply sucks and my life sucks more.

Gabriel is sixteen…almost seventeen. According to the judge who released him from the juvenile detention center, he has to be home by 8:00 every night. It's 10:30 and I have no idea where he is. I could call the police and have him arrested for violating his probation. If I did that, I would have to go to court and get an attorney. That would cost $3,000. I know this because I have done it before and I don't want to do it again. I am determined not to spend any more money on him beyond clothing and food. The next time the police pick him up, I will say, "Thank you very much, but please keep him." Sadly, he has not been arrested for several months … but he will be, and soon. Of this, I am certain.

And then he takes my money. And forty dollars is gone from my wallet. And I think, *he's such a moron. He's so blatant, so obvious.* And it's not like I didn't take money from my mother's purse. I did. But I never took all of her money. I took the loose change. I took a dollar. I took a few coins from the charity box—I didn't empty the whole box! And I realize that the dollar value of his crime is more than just an expression of inflation over the last thirty five years, it's a complete I-can-do-whatever-I-want-to-in-your-fucking-face slap in the face. He's an awful son-of-a-bitch, this son of mine, and it's so hard not to hate him while I love him.

And with forty dollars—my dollars—in his pocket, he skips out the front door to play with his friends. "Bye Mommy. Bye Dad," he says. "I'll see you later." He is sweetness and light, my thief of a son. And I wish he were a chameleon, but he is not. He is crazy.

I have these wonderful, horrible fantasies of his disappearance. And Paula thinks I'm sick. But I know people. I know people who make people disappear. They are not the bigger than life characters on smaller than life flat TV screens. They are respectable people who make things happen with a phone call. Buildings burn down. Warehouses become empty. Children disappear. I meet them in the clubhouse at my country club. We share a cigar, a hot dog, and beer. I say, "I desperately need your help."

They say, "Rick. Baby. For you, anything." and we play another round of golf as little white balls fly over our heads. It's that simple.

This, now, is my defining moment. I know it! The last time I had Gabriel taken away, I let him come back. What a schmuck I was! I was indecisive. I was weak. I let love get in the way of preserving the eighty percent of my family that was worth preserving. Now, I think, even if I am caught, I am better off. I am free of this terrible burden in this cynical cynical world where love has no place and men of action and depth are rewarded with wonderful jobs and buckets of happiness. I want a job that is not just wonderful, but the fulfillment of all my professional aspirations. I want so much more than happiness. I want family bliss on a regular basis and that will never happen with Gabriel in my life. I have to be a man of action. I have to complete my life unencumbered.

So I say to my acquaintance on the putting green, as another white ball glides past the hole and into the high grass, "You can find him at the Wawa on Saturday night. He'll be the one sipping the super-sized raspberry Slushy." I am free.

But I can't. Not really. I can't carry out the dark fantasies that drive me to write this memoir. This is not my defining moment at all. I am weak and losing my wife to the cyber millionaire. It's April and my birthday is two weeks away and my beautiful long and thick and curly auburn hair is now grey and sparse. The sun is shining. The wind is blowing. The crocus is poking its purple head through the moist and loose soil. In less than five hundred days Gabe will be eighteen; I will be fifty-one. I will have another half dozen crows feet extending from the watery corners of my eyes to the dry cheek bones that rest diagonally above the soon-to-be wrinkled corners of my mouth. I will have added two pounds of girth to my body, as has been my pattern every year for the last fifteen years. I will step on the scale and cringe. I will leave my bedroom, walk down the hall, open the white door with the thick black crack down its middle, the result of a swift right hook meant to punctuate a moment of fourteen-year-old rage, and walk into the chaos that is Gabriel's room. I will find him sleeping and I will ask myself, "Should I kiss him or kick him?" And that will define my day, but never my life. I am the bastard poet of hell's damnation—totally screwed, totally confused, and totally in search of my rightful claim to understand my position in the vast universe of love and hate.

Chapter 7

There is something about him, something I fail to recognize or fully appreciate. Gabriel possesses a six-month-old intensity that surprises me. At night, when I put him to bed, when I hold him in my arms or rock him to sleep, everything seems perfect. Then I lay him down in his crib and within seconds the wailing begins. The gentle transition from the safety of my arms to the solitude of his crib has altered his temperament. It seemed odd to me that he won't be put down, that every attempt to provide him with rest ends in crying. Nonetheless, we follow Dr. Ferber's good advice. We go back to the room. We reassure our baby. Paula sings to him. But ultimately, we have no choice but to let him cry himself to sleep despite the urge to comfort him throughout the night. And every evening, without fail, the situation repeats itself. At the moment of separation, he cries for what seems like a very long time, until the weight of his own exhaustion breaks him down and knocks him out. Paula says it's normal, but I have my doubts. Yet when he falls asleep, he is usually out for the night.

I don't recall at what age the crying stopped, but I do recall that he was always docile in my arms, usually asleep until that moment—the transition—when the warmth of my body was replaced by the warmth of a blanket. His inability to put himself to sleep would be an issue for him as a toddler, a child, an adolescent and an adult. And his inability to transition from one situation to another would show itself in nearly everything he did.

Once we were playing a game. I'll call the game *Climbing Daddy*. Daddy lies on the floor and one-year-old Gabriel climbs over me. I'm on my back. I'm staring at the ceiling. I hear childish laughter and movement and feel tiny hands and pointy knees working their way across my chest. It's fun. There's a lot of energy in the room and Gabriel quickly traverses my forty-four-inch chest. Within seconds he is up, over, and back on the floor, proud of his conquest—Mt. Rick. So he readies himself to scale my body again. He turns himself around, grabs my shirt and pulls himself up to my chest. The view from Mt. Rick is not so interesting and his stay there is brief. It's just me, a lump of a body lying on the floor, and Gabriel, a bit of a muskrat scampering about. The game continues. Gabriel is hysterical laughing his magical laugh. He goes back and forth, over and over, up and down... all around. It's endless and so for a bit of diversity I roll on to my stomach. Now, instead of a blank ceiling to look at, my nose is pressed into a dirty beige carpet. Yet my climber is not deterred. He is the opposite; he is determined to conquer me again and again. It's almost like he can't stop, as if stopping would admit one-year-old defeat. So I stop it for him. I stand up. I shake my body and watch little bits of dirt fall to the ground. And even though he is only one, I know what's coming: the wail—the scream—the I don't want to go to bed voice that we have grown accustomed to. It is the voice of transition.

Sixteen years later I am being interviewed by a psychiatrist named Robert Hershey. The interview is not a talk-show; it is a court-ordered psychiatric evaluation that costs me $1,000. A juvenile court judge, unable to understand my family dynamics, wants to know if Paula and I are sane. Separately, we are interviewed. Paula, the clinical psychologist, is utterly offended by the request. However, when the courts are involved, you do what you're asked to do.

Paula's interview takes place a week before mine. She had little to say about it, so I asked her how it went, knowing that like me there were hundreds of other things she would have rather been doing. I won't say that she was angry but her usually warm face had a stern look to it. She paused for a moment, as if she were about to say something important, and instead said this: "What a waste of time."

When it's my turn, I'm asked things about my childhood, my job, my marriage, whether I am happy, and whether or not I beat my children. When the evaluation is over, (I hope I pass) Dr. Hershey asks me one last question as I leave his office. He has interviewed Gabriel, too. He knows our situation. He said, "I've seen a lot of kids like Gabriel and I know that you and your wife have done what you can, but I always wonder what the breaking point is. From what I understand from speaking to you, your wife and Gabriel, his behavior was an issue long before you sent him away. Did you ever think it would reach a point where sending him away was the only option?"

I was tired. I was angry. I didn't want to tell him any more than was necessary for the evaluation. I said, "No. I never thought it would come to that. I always thought he was a smart kid who would figure it out." I lied.

●

There is temperament and there is fear. When Gabriel was three we planned an elaborate birthday party in our backyard. Lots of kids, their parents, and an assortment of friends and family came to celebrate Gabriel's third year of life. I spent hours making an amazing cake that looked like a train. Its smoke stack was a Tootsie Roll, its wheels were Oreo cookies and its windows were Gummy Bears. I was as proud of my cake as I was of Gabriel.

When it became time to sing Happy Birthday, Gabriel was playing in the basement with a friend.

"Gabriel, it's time to come outside," I said.

"No."

"Come on, Gabriel, everyone is waiting."

"No."

"Gabriel, don't you want your presents?"

"No."

"Gabriel. I mean it. Now! Let's go!"

"No."

Paula was waiting for us in the yard. She won't be happy. So I picked him up and got the transition voice. He was barely three, but I was used to it. I slung him over my hip as his feet and arms attempted to swim away and his voice registered its full stride. Was he stubborn or scared? People were waiting. People had expectations. Grandparents, aunts, uncles and cousins were ready to record this monumental event for posterity. But Gabriel wasn't about to budge.

No surprises: I knew his moods, his ways, his voice of love and hate and three-year-old desperation. I loved him so much—my miracle boy—that I forgave most everything he did that brought a question to my mind. He's only three, right? I can put him down and leave him to play with his friend and everyone who loves him will continue to do so. And that's what I did despite my embarrassment. And I cut his cake alone in the kitchen, and I distributed its parts to our hungry guests, and not once did I think that a precedent was being established.

Two years later, Gabriel is graduating from pre-school. The ceremony is adorable as we watched thirty little people, dressed to the nines, their blue paper mortarboards desperately clinging to their heads, march in a row toward the stage. Parents, siblings and grandparents filled a small auditorium. My camera was positioned on a tripod beside a dozen others ready to record this five-year-old rite of passage. There was no valedictorian. There were no speeches. There were only songs to be sung and diplomas to be presented as one by one the children made their way to the stage, where they stood for the national anthem.

The last child in the processional was Gabriel. He walked alone, ten feet behind the line of bobble-head boys and girls. As the other children lined up on the stage, shoulder-to-shoulder, Gabriel chose to keep the distance between himself and the others. He was sitting alone. He was ignoring his friends. These were not children he disliked; these were his pals and most of them had been to our house. Gabriel was very popular. But that didn't matter. His very being was anathema to being singled out or observed.

Twenty-nine children smiled and grinned and jostled each other during fifteen minutes of songs and five minutes of reading names. Some of the children hammed it up and some of them simply grinned and beared it, and one child, my child, sat apart from the group at the far end of stage right, his arms crossed over his chest, his face, determined and miserable.

At home, it was not the best world either. The transitional voice has turned into a temper. It surfaced when Gabriel was three and never went away. Once, when he was five we put him in a plastic time-out chair for misbehaving. He picked up the chair, flung it across the room, and broke off two of its legs. Honestly, I was impressed.

We think we learn from our mistakes but we don't. We think that we see a warning sign but we dismiss it. And when we realize it's too late, we ask ourselves over and over again, what if? Dr. Hershey asked the wrong question. Who cares about the breaking point? The breaking point was inevitable and could easily have been expressed in a number of ways. Something was bound to make us crack. Along the way was question after question after question in the evolution of Gabriel's behavior. Were we too strict? Were we too lenient? Did we force him into situations he was unprepared for? Was it us? Was it genetic? Was there something wrong with a six-year-old boy who refused to get out of the car to attend his karate birthday party even though he asked for it and thirty of his friends were waiting for him?

Here's what didn't work: Ritalin, Adderall, Paxil, Trileptal, Lamictal, Zyprexa, Risperdal. The list goes on. And let's not forget play therapy. Talk. Talk. Talk. But once when Gabriel was eight there was a two-week reprieve. It was drug induced and it was wonderful. It was everything Gabriel, baggage excluded, good and great coming to the surface.

"Gabriel, it's time to do your homework," I said.

"Okay, Dad. I'll do it now," and he did. Wow!

The change was instant and obvious and we thought, holy shit, finally something was working. He was years from his worst behavior, but even at eight the stress was mounting. A day did not go by that wasn't punctuated by incidents large and small.

But this new pill, this miracle drug, had changed everything. And falling asleep was fine, as the ugly punctuation marks of his life simply disappeared.

A day goes by. Another day passes. A week is upon us and still he is an angel. This is the real Gabriel, the boy we knew he could be. But was this really happening? Were we really out of the woods? Sadly, the answer was no. The impact of the drug was eventually countered by the power of the human spirit, and Gabriel's spirit is a powerful force of nature.

We had not fully accepted that he was changed forever but it was hard to ignore the facts. He sat at the table for dinner. He sat in the classroom to learn. He went to bed. Thank God he went to bed. And *no* was apparently disappearing from his vocabulary.

Two weeks from the day that he began his new medication, he was playing at a friend's house. His friends were all nice kids. It was one of the things that always made me feel good about Gabriel. They came from good families. The parents of his friends were our friends. They were smart and polite and they all liked Gabriel. So when I arrived to pick him up, knowing of his transformation, I expected nothing more than to quietly leave. Gabriel and his friend were playing with Legos. It was dinner time. It was time to go, time to transition.

The details aren't important. What's important to understand is that everything fell apart. It was physically and mentally impossible for Gabriel to stop what he was doing and walk away. What started out as a mere no, evolved into a shriek that transformed into a fight that led me to drag my tear-filled son back to my car. Eventually, he recuperated although the scene would repeat itself many times in the years to come.

I often wonder what they were thinking in Pompeii, that beautiful Italian city destroyed in an instant, covered in ash and buried for centuries. Surely, the people of the first century noticed a little smoke coming out of Mt. Vesuvius. Yet their lives went on. They didn't run away. They were artists and merchants and farmers, who, for all of their days, lived in the shadow of the volcano , never knowing when their world would end, and perhaps never expecting it either. And that's what it's like living with a volcano.

Chapter 8

A little boy is so much better than a dog and gets just about as much attention as a puppy. When I had a puppy, I liked to take him out and show him off. When I had a little boy, I felt the same way. When the puppy got older I took him on my runs, the two of us jogging side-by-side. Although I don't have a dog anymore, I do have Gabriel. I know that doesn't sound right, but I took great pleasure in running with my dog and even more pleasure in running with Gabriel. He loved it too.

I strapped my baby boy into a large pink three-wheeled stroller designed to move swiftly through the streets, over the curbs and around the potholes. It was one of our favorite things to do. I could see and feel his joy as off we went on our runs. There was no fear at all as I ran through town with my grinning little boy, his mop of wild red hair blown back in the breeze. He giggled. He talked. He asked me to go faster and I did.

I was sure that one day I would have a running partner or a biking partner or at least this person that would always want to do things with me. Perhaps Gabriel thought the same way. After all, when he was two we were inseparable. Wouldn't it have been wonderful to hold on to that wish? Two-year-old wishes, even in adults, are treasures we should hold in our hearts forever.

●

I am forgetting to breathe. It is a phenomenon I don't understand. I can be sitting in my car or watching television or doing laps in the pool when all of a sudden, and for no particular or discernible reason I am out of air. It blows me away. It frightens me. So I breathe with the foreknowledge that if I don't, I die. I do it once, deeply. I do it again, more so. I know that the blood coursing through my lungs will carry oxygen to the furthest reaches of my capillaries, ensuring a mental state that will remind me to breathe again and again and again.

Breathing is an act that every other living thing does without thought. But it's not working that way for me. I don't know why I'm consumed by a lack of oxygen. I walk: right foot, left foot, right foot, left foot. I talk: *How are you today, Gabriel? Can we pretend to get along, and not strangle each other?* I postulate grand thoughts in my head without ever thinking that I must be thinking. Yet thirty or forty seconds pass and I realize again that I have forgotten to sustain my life through oxygen. So I take a breath—my breath, the breath—a long and thoughtful inhalation, feeling the muscles in my chest expand and contract as I take in the invisible elixir of life—air. I hold it, wrapping my blood and lungs around its invisible nature. I luxuriate in the process, exhaling slowly, preserving my sense of survival, hoping that this conscious effort becomes an unconscious pattern of normalcy.

And then, of course, I realize the problem: I am not normal. Not me. Not my life. Not my family, dysfunctional or otherwise. It began with the inability to conceive. That singular failing separated me from normal people, regardless of the fact that it was ultimately conquered. Like my inability to breathe, unique in its own sad way, my distinction from the universe of young married men who procreated with ease, marked me for life. Creating life, like breathing, was a natural thing. Yet my failure to do either without conscious intervention leads me to believe that my infertility and my failure to breathe automatically are somehow related. That perhaps my forgetfulness is an expression of the strange path my life is on, and understanding the etiology of my condition does little to alleviate the aching journey.

I tell no one, especially Paula. How can I? What would I say? "Honey, I can't breathe." *Deep breath.* "Honey, I'm so forgetful. Would you please pass the oxygen?" *Deep breath.* "Honey, why is our life such an awful nightmare? How did this happen to us?" *Deep breath—deep breath—deep breath.*

My condition is getting worse. It is expressing itself in a loud panting noise at each actualization of emptiness in my lungs. People stare; I breathe; I pant.

When did this begin? I'm not sure. Maybe it began with a miracle? Gabriel was a miracle once. I know that you know that. I know it too. I readily admit it—big fucking deal! Big fucking woop! What is he now? I think you know. I think the painful truth of the matter is that he is still a miracle and that is why I hate him so much.

Once upon a time he was born. *Breathe. Breathe. Breathe.*

We placed an ad. We got a phone call. We met a girl who couldn't raise her baby. So we said, "Okay. We'll do it for you."

And she said, "Okay. That's cool."

And for four months we took her to the doctor's. We bought her nice things like clothes and an air conditioner. We met her family and friends. Her mother seemed nice until she asked us for $5,000 for the baby. How could she do that? How could we do that? *Breathe.* We couldn't/wouldn't do that. It wasn't the money, it was the principle. We never wanted a child of ours to think that we got him or her for the right price. And we got him on the cheap. We really did. And now it's $150,000 later, and that doesn't even include attorney fees. *Breathe. Breathe.* And those poor people who gave our son life; they had nothing. They had a house with a door and couch and an empty refrigerator and walls that peeled, and an offer to feed a mouth that they couldn't feed, so they took it.

And we...me....I...was the rescuer of Gabriel from the impoverishment of Camden, New Jersey. A frightening city overrun by children in a landscape like none we had ever seen growing up in suburbia. Surrounded by communities of affluence, Camden is a formerly thriving industrial town of broken and empty row houses and graffiti covered school yards. It is a place where death fractures the worlds of the young people least prepared to cope.

So there! I saved him, and I loved him, and I gave him comfort and joy. And for my reward I get kicked and spat upon and abused. *Breathe. Breathe.*

●

It is two weeks before Gabriel is due to be born. Paula is sleeping, her body covered in a gold paisley sheet, tattered at the corners. Casey, our beautiful Siberian husky, is resting at the foot of the bed. They are breathing in unison, breathing as one, neither confronted with my forgetfulness or my inability (past or present) to breathe. Paula's body rises slightly with each breath. Casey's fur, a dark grey like an impending storm, lifts gently as she breathes in and out. I am thinking I need some air. I take it in slowly, consciously. It's good to breathe.

In the morning I will give away my dog. She can't be trusted. She snarls and bites, and as much as I love her, I can't take the risk that she might harm the baby that I am expecting to bless our home. When Casey became part of the family, she was eight years old. She belonged to a friend of a friend of a friend, who one day realized that a small apartment wasn't the place for a dog bred to run. So I picked up Casey at the apartment and brought her to our small home with the small back yard. I decided that since the kid thing wasn't working out, that I might as well have a dog. Huskies like to run; I like to run. It seemed like a good match, this, our first adoption.

Casey had a brown eye and a blue eye and an attitude and a temper and fun-loving spirit I adored. When she was wonderful, she was wonderful. When she was not, we hid in the closet, not quite sure what to do with the rabid dog in our house.

I remember the day we brought her home. I played in the yard and took her for a run. Later that evening I found her under a small table in our bedroom that Paula and I used for a night stand. In her mouth she had a sock. When I approached her to get her out from under the table and retrieve the sock, she snarled at me. She bared her teeth as if the sock was her baby and I was threatening to break-up the family.

"Casey," I implored in a soft voice, the voice of a parent gently guiding a young child to the logical conclusion of a simple predicament. "Come on, sweetie. Give it to me. Give me the sock, baby." More teeth. More snarling. Heavy breathing. (Her, not me.) "Come on," I said again. "It's okay. You don't have to be afraid." Nothing but teeth. *Deep breath. Deep breath.* (Me, not her.) For a while I try the gentle approach without any luck.

Then I said, "Casey!" in a loud and stern voice of a demanding father who expects obedience. "Casey! Give me the sock! Give it to me now! GIVE! ME! THE! SOCK!" I screamed.

It was our first fight and I was losing. She snarled. She snapped. She did a masterful job of frightening me and Paula.

That night Casey slept under the nightstand while Paula and I slept on the pull out sofa in the living room. We left the bedroom, closed the door and locked it. In the morning, when we woke, I cautiously opened the bedroom door and noticed the sock lying on the floor. I called out to Casey and she came running toward me, apparently pleased to see me, and pleased to have established her dominant position in the family. There was no doubt about who would be the alpha dog.

Over time we realized that Casey was crazy. She had her moods, but if we left her alone, she didn't bother us. And so a shoe, a bra, an old t-shirt, anything soft and loose could easily end up as the object of her affection, and we were dammed to ever retrieve that object until she was ready to let it go.

For the most part, she was affectionate and adoring. She was a man's dog: big but not too big, a little wild, a little dangerous. She liked to run, she liked to play and, when I needed it, she was there for a hug or a pat or a kiss.

But she had this thing, this crazy dangerous side. One day, I found her under the kitchen table with my underwear. I don't know why, but after nearly three years I was getting tired of *the thing*. Couldn't she trust me? Couldn't she see that we loved her? I would never hurt this beautiful animal. Never! But I tired of the nonsense and went after her with the intent of winning.

I screamed, "Gimme my god-damn underwear!" meeting her glare, eye to eye.

Her lips rose above her teeth, exposing long pointed incisors meant to rip living meat. She snarled in a low breathless monotone, like an animal in the bush waiting for its prey. "I want my fucking underwear!" I insisted, totally oblivious to my own flaring nostrils and tortured breathing. It didn't matter what I did. We had been down this road many times before and the outcome was always the same. She wins. I lose.

And so I did the unthinkable. I was young and invincible and I'd had it with this bitch. I reached for the underwear as fast as I could, fast enough I thought, to catch her off guard and pull it away. Casey did what any crazy dog would do. She instantly ripped open my palm with her sharp teeth. It was so quick that I barely saw her move as my blood spewed across her face, my hand and the blue linoleum floor.

"Shit," I screamed, grabbing my hand as the pain seared up my arm. *I'm such an idiot. What the fuck was I thinking?* Dog versus human...dog wins. *Breathe. Breathe.* I reached for a towel to clean the blood and examine the wound. It was bad. It was deep. It was painful.

Casey was immobile and emotionless. She was still under the table, still had my underwear, and seemed to be completely oblivious of the agony on my face.

I found a piece of paper and a pencil, and with my bloody right hand I held down the paper, and with my left hand I scribbled a note to Paula that said, *Casey bit me. At the hospital for stitches. Love, Rick.*

As Gabriel's birth approached, as our salvation became closer to becoming our son, we knew we couldn't keep Casey in the house. There had just been an incident in the news where a husky went into a crib and killed a baby. Evidently, some huskies find newborns to be threatening. The lunacy and biting aside, that one story was enough to convince us that Casey had to go.

We found a home with a boy and yard, and although we told Casey's new owners that she could be temperamental, we never told them exactly how temperamental she could really be. They would come for Casey and for the third time in her life she would have a new family.

I seemed to be breathing fine when the doorbell rang. I could see the father through the sidelight window. He was older than I, slightly grey, with a large belly and a friendly face. I could see the boy, too. He was blonde and eager and brimming with excitement. The boy looked to be about ten years old. He was the same age as Casey.

I opened the door and introduced them to her, the father having met her once before when I brought Casey to his house a few days earlier. I gave the boy her bowl and her leash and I said my goodbye to the dog that had loved me, hated me, maimed me and enabled me to take my mind off, in temporary spurts, the sadness that segregated me from being normal.

Breathe, I thought. I had to breathe. In a few weeks I would be a father and Paula would be a mother. A baby was coming to my house to stay forever. A baby is so much better than a dog. *Breathe*, I told myself again. Don't forget. And I wanted to, I wanted desperately to breathe, but all I could do was weep. So I wept a few barrels of salt water, totally unaware of the breathing that accompanied my tears or the signals that an unspeaking and invisible God was sending to me. How did I not see the signs? Were forty days of rain a sign? Was turning a river into blood a sign? How about parting the Red Sea? How about a dozen stitches to sew my hand back together? A sign? If only I knew what was coming.

Chapter 9

I want to thank God for ruining my life, for taking what little bit of pleasure I might have had in this universe and converting it to crap. Thank you, truly, for everything. I mean let's face it; I have no one else to blame, so I might as well blame Him or Her or It. And I want to thank Him, Her or It for being so Goddamn obvious. If it's all about signs and wonders—thunder—lightning—floods and shit, then I missed every one. Here's one sign I missed: Seven miscarriages. Here is another sign I missed: violence. When I was in my early twenties I would have these horribly violent dreams. I was on a battlefield or in a car wreck or a witness to murder and maiming, and I could never understand where these dreams came from and why they were following me. It's so obvious now.

God is a fickle Entity, or at least a vengeful He, She or It. I think the Entity may be punishing me and here are the reasons why. My crimes: I have been a thief and on several occasions between the ages of seven and twelve, I did, in fact, steal many ten-cent packs of gum from the corner deli. I have been a liar: when I was sixteen I told my parents I was going to the movies one afternoon with my friend, Walter. I was, in fact, meeting seventeen-year-old Beth Swanson, who brought me to her house, kissed me for at least two hours and, before she brought me home, gleefully performed oral sex on a body whose singular goal was the immediate and constant gratification of anything sexual. I have been a cheat: As much as I enjoyed the constant attention of Beth Swanson, I also enjoyed the slightly less frequent but often more meaningful attention of Laura Burke, who happily (at least for me) took me all the way. I have been a beggar: in college I spent most of my loose money on beer and pot. I rarely had money for less important things like food. To remedy the situation,

I would beg for food in order to sustain my drunken stupor or alternate state. I begged my friends, my non-friends, and especially the pretty redhead who worked at Burger King who felt sorry for me at one in the morning when I would drag my altered state ass into the restaurant and, pathetically, albeit sweetly, worm my way into a Whopper and fries. I have been selfish: A few months before Laura Burke and I ran parallel lives to Beth Swanson and me, I joyfully, gleefully, willingly, ecstatically, and permanently, lost my virginity to Gretchen Goldstein. She too was seventeen to my sixteen. We were at a party at Jim Weston's house over Christmas break. Jim Weston, who, two weeks later would fall asleep at the wheel on his way home from a skiing weekend in the Poconos. In a dreamlike state he crossed Interstate 80 and kissed the grill of a sixteen-wheeler loaded with metal tubing from a factory in Wayne, New Jersey, just ten minutes from the exact spot where, unlike my bar-mitzvah, I really became a man. As Gretchen and I were leaving Jim's party, we went to the room where dozens of coats were piled high like giant ant hills of down, wool and cotton. They were black and red and purple and green—all the colors of a cold New Jersey winter. And there, upon the soft and lumpy and colorful mounds of winter coats, I somehow managed to enter the real world of real women. And it was quick. And it was glorious. And it was over almost as suddenly as it began. And people were banging on the door. People like us who wanted sex on dirty coats and smelly wool caps. And I pulled up my pants in adolescent glory of my ninety-second conquest, doing all that I could not to throw up from the beer, the carnal pleasure, and the smell of woman that in my mind covered me from head to toe but in fact swathed only my penis in olfactory delight. Gretchen was nonplussed. She had allowed herself to be my vessel, and did so without hesitation. Was there any pleasure for her? I never asked. She never told me. She said, "Okay, Rick, we better go now." And we did. And finally, I have been weak: I once saw a man beaten in a bus terminal and along with twenty other spectators did nothing, not one Entity damn thing. And He, She or It punished me. And for that, I probably deserved it.

If there is a God, it knows my soul. He, She or It, knows what I want. I want a family that embodies the antithesis of the house I grew up in. He, She or It says, "give it your best shot you liar, you cheat, you thief, you selfish son-of-a bitch. It won't be easy." Signs and wonders and punishment and no Goddamn hope. "You want hope?" He, She or It, informs me, "I am here to tell you that hope is a notion that is ruinous by nature."

And I remembered what I had hoped for in my life, what I prayed for, what seemed so simple for Him, Her or It to deliver to my doorstep. When I was seventeen I hoped that God would bring me a New Jersey state wrestling championship in the one hundred and eighty-eight pound weight class. God wouldn't have to do a lot because I was already pretty good and I had won twenty-one straight matches heading into the state tournament. I was ready, both physically and mentally. But was He, She or It? As I stepped on the mat, I discovered that He, She, or It and I, were not ready at all. Thirty seconds into my 22nd match, the reigning state champion proved to me that his relationship with the Almighty superseded my own. His signs were stronger and more obvious. Where I saw a rainbow, he saw a hurricane. Where I saw a dove, he saw a hawk. He knew his Him, Her or It better than I. In less than a minute I was pinned. I was decked. I was counting the lights on the ceiling of the Morris County College gymnasium. It was like I never even stepped out on the mat. I never shook his hand. I never jumped back as he grabbed my legs and sucked me in with his massive arms and turned me over and mangled me like a piece of clay crushed between the chrome bumpers of colliding Cadillacs. I never broke a sweat. My heartbeat barely rose. When it was over, I saw the universal disappointment in my father's eyes, my brother's face, and my coach's body language—I would not be his first state champion. I would be no one's champion.

Now my arms are wrapped around Gabriel. He is fifteen and we are wrestling, but not for sport. He wants to run away and for some strange reason I want to keep him home. At each turn, he finds another exit until I determine that the only way to keep him in the house at one in the morning is to tackle him. There is no referee. My advantage is weight and strength and size. His advantage is youth and speed and refusal. He refuses to lose—ever! Every fight, every match, ever scuffle, every unpleasant conversation or request, no matter its origin, is ultimately about winning. Clinically, it's called Oppositional Defiant Behavior. I also have a clinical term for his behavior. I call it being an asshole. Gabriel likes to win—so do I! Of course, there is never a winner. Never! Never! Never! And although I am able to keep him home this time, there is no sense of victory.

All I really want is for him to go to school, but that is becoming less of an option. Remarkably, four weeks have passed since the aforementioned wrestling match and he has not missed a single day since then. It's the longest stretch of not missing school since September and now it is May. It's unlikely that the streak will last much longer, especially since I just found a six-pack of Coca-Cola in his school back-pack. I tell him he can't take the soda to school and he tells me to go fuck myself.

Oh my God! Here we go again. His anger is instantaneous. He was up and ready and all set to go and it appears as if I have ruined his streak.

I said, "Put the soda back."

He said, "Fuck you," again and again and again, and like so many times before I lost all perspective. What could have been a quiet morning turned into another ugly confrontation. Why should I care about *this* in the universe of Gabriel? This is nothing. This is six cans of coke that he wants to share with his friends to impress them. Maybe if he asked me I would have said yes, but I doubt it. It's just another excuse to hate each other.

So what could I do? I strip the back-pack from his hands and hold it tightly, as if letting go would end my life.

I say, "Go to school." And as I do he rips into me with a verbal onslaught. The words, the awful words, carefully selected to poison my heart, spew from his mouth as easily as water from a faucet.

We are standing eyeball to eyeball in the foyer by the front door.

His anger is unstable while mine is focused. The only question is who will explode first. The answer is me. I wrap my arms around him in a bear-hug, pick him up and carry his flailing body out of my house. I take two giant steps through the front doorway, arching my back in order to keep his feet off the ground. And finally, I take three giant steps on to the grass and drop him on my dandelion-covered lawn where he continues to share with me his sense of outrage.

"Fuck you, I'm not going to fucking school," he screams as he pulls out a cigarette, walks away and gives me the finger. Meanwhile, the little yellow school bus pulls up in front of our house—our lovely house in our lovely suburban neighborhood, where lovely children ride their colorful bikes, jump on their backyard trampolines, and rarely pay attention to mom and dad getting high in the Jacuzzi.

The bus driver, no stranger to picking up Gabriel, assesses the situation and keeps on driving. "Wait!" I scream, as if hailing a policeman to arrest the man who has just stolen my brand new high definition flat screen television that up until a few minutes ago hung gracefully over my fireplace like a treasured piece of art. And to my amazement she stops.

"Fuck you," screams Gabriel for effect, like I hadn't heard him the first fifty times.

"Get on the bus, or I'll call the police," I scream back. And amazingly he gets on the bus. I watch the folding glass door close behind him as he steps on board to find his seat. I see the bus drive away. And maybe this time I really did win…but I doubt it. He will be back; it's only a matter of time.

I go to work. I go to lunch. I'm sitting in a Thai restaurant in a very fancy mall in the wealthiest county in New Jersey that also happens to be the wealthiest county in the United States. The interior of the restaurant is green and decorated with unfinished paintings of Thai gods and kings and queens and other monuments that I suppose one might recognize if one were from Thailand. Of course, the paintings are supposed to be unfinished, it is a style or statement or something artistic that I fail to appreciate. The exterior wall of the restaurant, which is actually an interior wall of the mall, is glass from floor to ceiling. It is easily twelve feet high and forty feet long, and from where I sit I see everything within and without. I see a short chubby waiter place a triangular blue plate of chicken Pad Thai on my table. I see him fill my glass with water and then walk away. I see a woman go to an ATM machine to retrieve some cash. At first she looks to be fifty-ish like me. She is slender and has a nice face. But then she walks right by me, right by my table next to the glass wall, and I see her hands. Her hands are speckled and dry and eerily translucent like a crisp but wrinkled piece of rice paper. She is not fifty-ish, she is older and spotted and doing her best to conceal the truth. And the other women—the women who don't work—the women who don't have to because they have the good fortune to live in the wealthiest county in New Jersey, which happens to be the wealthiest county in the United States—they are walking, too, with purpose. Their bodies are tight and their clothing clings to them like unripe banana peels, just a little too tough.

I slurp a long rubbery noodle, its spicy brown sauce gently, pleasurably, burning my lips. I wipe my mouth with a rough cloth napkin. I see something else, something more than these women whose faces are taut and bodies are tight beyond the results of their middle-age exercise machines. I see a young woman in loose clothing, totally out of place in this upscale mall for the over-exercised and affluent. Her hair is black and long and messy and maybe not even washed in several days. She doesn't care. She doesn't notice that others notice her. She is joyfully out of place.

She has a child in her arms, an infant. The child is silky white and has messy black hair just like the mom. And the mom is dancing. And the infant is dancing too. And the mom holds the baby at arm's length. And she twirls. And she spins through the wide marble-floored hallways of the mall, where tiny subliminal halogen lights force passers-by to turn their eyes to the unknown objects of their desire. She lifts the baby up and down, occasionally pulling her son or daughter close to her. She kisses the baby on its neck and belly and tiny baby toes. And I cannot hear them through the glass, I can only see them. And what I see is what I had—a miraculous joy, an unfathomable bond, a magical connection bound by laughter. They are laughing, too; I see it. They are spinning and laughing and dancing and floating in a private space in their private universe in the middle of the mall where small but brilliant lights illuminate everything but them.

I am overcome with an urge, a visceral urge to scream at the mom, to eclipse her joy with the raw possibility that her baby, like my baby, has the undeniable possibility to bury hope. I want to warn her. I want her to know that we are victims of unconditional love. Stop while you can! Walk away! End the dance!

But she twirls away in her grey cotton sweats, past the looks of the taut-skinned tight-bodied, elderly ladies of the mall. They see her but fail to recognize her enigmatic situation. Her predicament is invisible but not to me. I am the devil and her happiness is an aberration for me to fix. I could do it in a scream that would shatter the glass wall between us. I could warn her but I don't.

So I look for a sign because that's what I do. I look and pray... for the mom, for the baby, and for my epiphany to arrive.

●

There have been moments when Gabriel made me proud. When my father-in-law died, he was the first to head to Florida to be with Paula and her mother. He had just turned sixteen. When he arrived, he hugged his grandmother and told her that he loved her. As I thought about his ability to comfort others, I realized that this was a strength of Gabriel's built upon a need to be needed. Throughout his life, in situations like this, Gabriel shined. How did I not realize this before? The boy who would not let us love him, desperately wanted to show his ability to love and comfort others. If he couldn't show love for his mother and father, then certainly he could muster up affection for his extended family and his other family, the family in his mind—his friends. He was always there for his friends.

At the funeral I sat in the second row of pews. Paula was with her brothers and her mother on the other side of the aisle, and Ethan, Jonathan and Gabriel sat directly in front of me. The eulogies were wonderful. Paula's father had a full life. He loved his family, his politics, his children and grandchildren. As Paula gave her eulogy she shared a story about the last time she spoke with her Dad less than two weeks before.

"And so I said to my Dad, you know, you really were a wonderful father. And he paused and looked back at me and said, *now you tell me?*"

That was Jim. He was sweet and honest and funny, and now that he was dead all of his shortcomings, whatever they might have been, were either forgotten or forgiven.

Gabriel and Jonathan cried through most of the service, as I kept passing them tissues to wipe their eyes and blow their noses. Ethan, the pragmatist, was sad, but not overwhelmed by his emotions.

We still had two more days in Florida before heading home. In some ways, our trip seemed like a mini vacation with a funeral dropped in the middle. We swam in the pool. We dined out. We buried Paula's dad. We entertained the long line of family and friends who stopped by to extend their condolences. A little stress? Sure. But that had been the tenor of most of our family vacations anyway.

For the most part, Gabriel was well behaved, but the longer we stayed the less tolerant he became of his brothers. He appointed himself the king of the television remote control, often bullying his brothers to watch only what he wanted. He was not a benevolent ruler; he was a despot. And I was the emperor whose patience was wearing thin. "Let them watch what they want," I screamed to no avail. But Gabriel couldn't do that. That was not how he ruled his kingdom.

He wanted more than just control of the TV. He wanted my cell phone. I said no. He wanted a new CD. I said no. He even started talking about the new car he expected me to buy him. No! No! No!

"Get a job," I begged him. "Get a job and you won't have to ask me for these things. Get a job and buy your own car."

"Fuck that," he said. "I want a fucking car. You said you would buy me a car," he screamed. And that is how the last two days in Florida went.

So just like when he was six and nine and thirteen and fifteen, he had done it again. He had swiftly negated all the good he had accomplished over the past week and forced me to focus on his venomous words and temper. And I thought, *please God; can you get me out of Florida?* The funeral had run its course and the mourning was over for me and my children. Please God, let me get back to work and away from this boy.

●

It was raining at the airport as we stood under a large cement awning waiting for the shuttle bus to take us from the car rental return to the airport terminal. We had had it. Paula was fried. I was exhausted. Even the kids were beat. A week of wear and tear on our emotions had finally caught up with Paula, me and the boys. It wasn't that life was so bad, it was just hard and unfair and unrelenting.

At the car rental return Paula saw Gabriel take a half smoked cigarette out of an ash tray and put it in his pocket, presumably to smoke at a later time.

"Gabriel," Paula said in disgust, "What are you doing?"

"Nothing," he said.

"Are you going to smoke that cigarette?" she pressed on. "Are you going to put that filthy cigarette that someone else had smoked and put in the trash, someone with germs you know nothing about… Are you going to put that disgusting cigarette in your mouth? How desperate are you?" she implored.

"Fuck you," he said. "Stay the fuck out of my life. I'll do what I want."

"What the hell is wrong with you," she said.

"I don't fucking care," he said. "I'll smoke whatever I want."

And that's when I stepped in.

"Of course, you will, Gabriel," I said, "because you're gross. What kind of a pig digs through the garbage for a used cigarette? You're a bully and a pig and I have had it."

And Gabriel said, "Fuck you, you piece of shit." And without hesitation I slapped him across the face, humiliating him in front of his brothers and all other bystanders. His muscles tensed and he raised his fists. He was threatening, always threatening, and his words were a blur of unrepeatable invectives. He wanted to strike me back, to break my nose, to kill me. So the cursing went on and on. As it did, I did what I had to and simply walked away. And as I turned my back, I felt his fist just above my kidneys.

"This is fine," I said as the shuttle bus pulled up. "Now I have something to tell Mr. Jackson." Jackson was Gabriel's probation officer and probably the only person who could influence his behavior. Mr. Jackson had the weight of the judicial system on his side and Gabriel knew it. Gabriel also knew that if he broke his probation (which could be anything from missing his curfew to stealing a pack of gum) he would have to go back to the Juvenile Detention Center. He also knew that the only way Mr. Jackson was going to find out anything was if Paula or I told him.

"Don't you tell Mr. Jackson shit," he said as he got on the bus still fuming.

"I'll tell him what I like," I said. "I'll tell him that you have been a bully, that you have been late on your curfew and that you have been threatening me and Mom." "I will slit your fucking throat," he said, completely oblivious to the middle aged couple sitting next to me.

"I will slit your throat and I will burn down your fucking house."

"And if I end up back in jail I will get a gun. And when I get out I will kill everyone. Don't think I won't do it, because I will. You better not say a fucking word to Jackson."

"Gabriel," I said. "Stop," but he didn't. He went on and on, repeating the many ways that he would kill me until finally even he was exhausted.

He kept on ranting and we said not a word, knowing from experience that our words would only exacerbate the situation. We were remarkably calm. At least that's what I thought. We knew we had helped to bring out the worst in him, but when the worst arrived we did not join in. We watched our lunatic son, waiting for the anger, as it often did, to subside.

I can only imagine what Gabriel's brothers were thinking. They were ten and twelve years old and were forced to process something they could not possibly understand. Yet how many times had they witnessed a scene just like this, and how many times did I ignore how it must have made them feel? It's not that I didn't care; it's just that my focus was to end the conflict and to do so with as little damage as possible. Keep them out of the fray. Be the interference. Make sure they are safe.

They were experienced witnesses to the crimes of Gabriel. They were worried and frightened and kept every ounce of their concerns to themselves. When I looked to see if they were safe, they were. Their bodies were unharmed. Yet who could measure the damage that was happening in their minds?

Twenty minutes later we were inside the terminal. Gabriel bought a box of chicken McNuggets at McDonald's and tapped me on the shoulder.

"Want a nugget," he said.

"No thanks," I answered.

●

He was never the angel of peace. He was the angel that foretold of the crumbling of the walls of Jericho. He was the angel that brought about war and he did not disappoint his God. At the age of sixteen he was formidable. Although average in height, his somber intensity made him appear much older. His muscular arms pulsed with an explosive energy aligned with his temperament and physicality. He was bigger and stronger than he had ever been. If only he could be wiser? If only he could be less blatant? But he was neither and now he was about to be caught again.

I was sitting in his room waiting for him to come up from breakfast. It was only 9:00 a.m. and it was unusual for him to be up so early on a Saturday. But he had plans, and when he had plans he was motivated.

I had plans too. I had plans to ask him about the four bottles of liquor wrapped tightly in a backpack in his closet. There were two bottles of whiskey, a bottle of wine and a bottle of gin. It was a nice little stash and of course the price was right—stolen from my liquor cabinet. But I didn't want a scene, especially now that Paula's grieving mother was staying with us.

"Why are you in my room?" Gabriel asked.

"We'll talk about this later," I said, and I tossed the empty backpack at him, having removed the bottles earlier and replaced the lock on the liquor cabinet.

"No we won't," he said.

"Yes, we will."

Gabriel's plans must have fallen through because a few hours later he was still in the house. Paula and her mother had gone out and had taken Ethan and Jonathan with them.

"So let me get this straight," I said. "You went into my nightstand. You took out the key to the liquor cabinet. You stole four bottles of my booze and then you put the key back. Does that pretty much summarize what happened?"

"I didn't steal anything," he said.

"Did it belong to you?" I asked.

"It was left over from a couple of years ago," he said emphatically.

"Gabriel, you're sixteen," I said. "Last time I checked the drinking age was 21. What were you going to do? Have a party with your friends?"

"No, it was just for me," he said.

"Bullshit," I replied.

And there he was all over again, little Gabriel in the park or the yard or the school...little Gabriel with his bag of toys and balls and trinkets. Be my friend and I'll let you play with my puppets. Do you want to see all the neat stuff I have in my bag? I've got some Jack Daniels that we can drink under the swings and a bottle of Cabernet for the sandbox.

"This is it," I said. "I have to tell Mr. Jackson."

"You can't tell Jackson," he said, his voice rising.

"Gabriel, this is an absolute violation of your probation."

"No!" he screamed. "Don't fucking tell him. I'm not going

back to jail."

"What am I supposed to do," I said. "I tell you what. You're grounded for a month."

"Fuck you," he said.

"Exactly. If I can't consequate this, then someone else will," I said as I walked away.

"Are you telling Jackson? Are you telling Jackson?" he said again and again. "Don't you tell him anything. Don't you fucking tell him shit. I swear to God I will kill you. He doesn't have to know this! I will slit your goddamn throat. You better not call Jackson. Are you calling Jackson? I mean it, I will kill you and hurt my brothers. I am not going back to jail."

I said nothing; there was nothing to be said. He was caged and I knew it and I didn't care. We were back on the bus in Florida. We were struggling again on the garage floor. It didn't matter where we were, it was always the same.

"Are you calling him? Are you calling Jackson?" he said again and again.

And he pushed me and I did not move. And he put his face in mine and I stood emotionless, unable to give him the satisfaction of either a yes or a no.

And he stepped back and he said, "I know you don't believe me." And slowly he walked toward the front wall of my bedroom. The one that has the three framed black and white pictures of my three handsome boys. And he faced the wall, and for a moment he turned to look at me. And then he looked at the wall once again, and in a flash of ferocity put his fist right through it, right beside the pictures of my most cherished treasures, right beside the head of Ethan.

And I said, as calmly as if I had asked him for a glass of milk, "Do you plan to fix that hole." He said nothing, intent on making his point. He walked away, not looking at me or the fist size hole in the wall. And I knew, as I have known for all these years, that there are no happy endings. There is life and passion and will and forgiveness, and a love of all things great and horrible.

●

It's late. It's dark. I'm tired. My mind is spinning. It's always spinning now, never focused like it once was. I think about work. I think about the woman in the mall and her wonderful happiness. I think about Gabriel and all the other shit that goes on or went on or will happen or never happened or will be imagined until that one day when the earth suddenly stops spinning and everything flies off into space except for me and him. We are tied to the biggest giant Sequoia tree in California and even gravity can't throw us off the planet—our roots are too deep. And Gabriel touches my hand and looks at me squarely with his wonderful black eyes, encrusted in the rich sand color of his face, and says, "Thank you."

And I say, "It's okay. You'll always be my favorite asshole."

This is our story, signs and wonders and all.

Chapter 10

L ook at this place. Look at me. I'm working out on a machine that lets me row for hours on end without ever traveling an inch. It's hardly dissimilar to the treadmill that enables me to run in place, or the stationary bike that tells me I have traversed twelve miles when in fact I never left the mirrored room where I am accompanied by other men and women who want to get fit but are wary of streets and cars and puddles and other dangers moving about in the un-air-conditioned world. There are beautiful people in very tight clothes who remind me of a past I might someday recapture if indeed I could reverse time. And there are other people in not so tight clothes that are not so beautiful who remind me that at least I am not them, not yet. I am in the middle, long past my past but far enough away from the inevitable future that I have not yet reached the stage of complete disgust with my body. I am happy in the sanitized world of the fitness center where there are constant reminders encouraging me to clean my sweat off the exercise machines at that very moment of completion, when slowly and painfully I lift my body from one or another rubber seat and move on to the next aerobic activity.

I seem to have developed a relationship with these machines that is more than platonic. There is an emotional connection. They push me harder and harder and I like that. I especially enjoy the rowing machine and the smooth flow of the flywheel creating resistance with each strenuous pull of its makeshift oars. I feel it in my arms and my back. I feel a twinge and a burn that is a bit of joyful pain. It reminds me of my challenge and my quest—to valiantly fight off the inevitable and willfully prevent that which is all too obvious: aging and death, although not necessarily in that order.

The fitness center is a very large room with people and

mechanisms and devices both large and small, each designed to shape or reshape or, in my case, retro shape my body into a form it hasn't possessed in nearly thirty years. When I looked the way that I would like to look today, I exercised in my garage with a crappy set of cement filled weights that my father bought me at Sears. There were only a few public gyms back then and they were dirty sweaty places where real boys idolized real men, and where torn and ragged shirts rarely matched grey-stained cotton sweat shorts. They were places of dust and grime and sweat, where old men with sagging muscles hung on to their youth like drowning sailors reaching for a lifeline. Women were not invited. These men were my heroes, clad in muscles, veins ready to burst, beer bellies, and leathered skin that draped their bodies in mystery. They were noble in their intensity and their desire to preserve their bulging biceps covered in middle-aged fat.

I was fifteen when I first set foot in a real gym. I weighed one hundred and fifty pounds and I could bench press one hundred and thirty-five. Three years later, on the precipice of manhood, and at one hundred and ninety-five pounds, I had no trouble doing several repetitions with a three hundred pound bar.

I sometimes take Gabriel to the fitness center (even though I still call it a gym) and occasionally we bench-press together. It's an interesting exercise in exercising. I'm not really into weightlifting anymore even though it's highly recommended for men and women of my age. Mostly, I stare at the monitor on the rowing machine and let it tell me all sorts of interesting things while Gabriel supposedly lifts weights out of my sight. For example, it tells me the rate of strokes I pull per minute. My stroke per minute rate is thirty-eight. It seems kind of slow in the universe of stroking, but to be honest, I'm not accustomed to counting my strokes, at least not where stroking really matters. Still, at my current rate of stroking, I will travel six thousand meters in thirty minutes and, according to the monitor I will burn three hundred and twenty eight calories on my journey to nowhere.

What the monitor doesn't tell me is what I really want to know.

What I really want to know is what will happen if I walk up to the girl on the Stairmaster in front of me, the girl with the amazing ass that goes up and down with each slow and presumably painful step. I watch the sweat trickling down her back. I watch her as she walks where I row, on a trip to nowhere. I'm mesmerized by the fluidity of her motion as small streams of sweat break away from the bottom of her shirt and cross that area of exposed skin between her shirt and her tights, over the large blue and gold butterfly tattoo at the small of her back, and just above the spot where her thong descends into that area where, from my vantage point, five feet behind her and two feet below her, my eyes are drawn. Oh, monitor, do you think that she will give me her phone number? Oh, monitor, will she be oblivious to the growing number of soft brown spots on my arms and legs? Will she not notice my expanding paunch or the diagonal wrinkles that extend out from the corners of my eyes? Do something amazing, oh, amazing rowing machine and all knowing monitor. Fulfill my fantasy. Tell me that when I'm done with my six thousand meter journey (the one that requires one thousand one hundred and forty strokes) that in addition to ending up precisely where I began, that, at least, for the sake of my fragile fifty-year-old ego, I will get the girl: the girl with the great ass, with the butterfly that taunts me, and the wonderfully sweat-stained tights. Is that really too much to ask?

"What the fuck are you looking at?" says Gabriel, as he sneaks up behind me, knowing full well what I'm looking at. Then he gives me a look (you pathetic bastard) and says, "Give it up, old man." As if he knows something I can't or won't admit: I will never get any closer to that ass than I am at this moment. I will never touch it with anything more than my mind. I will never press my body against hers. And then he smiles (the smug little shit) and I smile, too, because I know he is right.

"Fuck you," I say with a grin, like a buddy sharing a joke, knowing full well the verbal landmine I am exposing. Yet I also know that this is what it has come to, this pleasure, this rare moment, this veritable mind-meld, a couple of guys who really don't like each other, sharing something as special as a rainbow or a sunset. And even though I am incredibly disciplined at the gym—and even though Gabriel is incredibly undisciplined at the gym—and even though I know that after he did a set of bench presses he went outside to have a smoke, I don't care. Why should I? Smoking won't kill him, it takes too long. Something else will kill him, something I don't like to think about. A gun. A car. An angry girlfriend. A cop. Me. But it doesn't matter because we just shared an amazing-ass moment, and how often do a father and son get to do that? A father and son who have fallen so far apart, who have fought and exchanged blows. If we are, in fact, going to kill each other some day, shouldn't we at least share one of the most sublime pleasures that the Deity had the good sense to create, the wonderfulness that is a woman's body? So we did, and I smiled and he laughed and he adjusted his shorts and bent over and smacked me on the side of the head.

This is poetry. This is art. This is the human condition, transcending all animosity. Do I care that my brief obsession has objectified this person? That I have endorsed, in my own quiet way, a sexist thought for the sake of thirty seconds of bonding with my son. Of course, not! I was sixteen once and Gabriel is sixteen now, and there are certain memories and father/son traditions that all the political correctness in the world cannot remove from our genetic code. If the appreciation of a great ass is not top among these, then surely the viability of the human species is doomed.

A great ass is a living monument to beauty in a culture destined to crush our appreciation of form. This great ass moment occurred because a father and a son chose to forget that they would prefer to see each other dead. Instead we chose to set aside our hatred in favor of our mutual respect for classic beauty. I should have kissed that ass in gratitude.

Back in the car, I smelled cigarette smoke and pizza. It's an unusual combination since smoking has been banned from all restaurants—another infringement on our civil liberties, the right to slowly poison ourselves to death. So now I know that in addition to smoking a cigarette between each set of exercises, Gabriel also managed to fit in a few slices of pizza with money that no doubt was stolen from my wife's purse when she left it unattended. I see that he's got a little bit of tomato sauce on his cheek and without warning I reach over to erase the red stain from his face.

I obviously caught him off guard because the first thing he does is instantly pull back and scream, "What the fuck!"

"Take it easy," I say. "You've got tomato sauce on your face."

"Don't fucking touch me," he says, turning an angry gaze to a simple gesture offered by one of the few people on the planet that still loved him.

What a jerk, I think to myself. What an incredible jerk.

And then I wonder how he would have reacted if instead of me it was the girl with the amazing ass. I see her in my mind gliding toward him. It's not hard to do; he is often surrounded by girls. The young Venus sits beside him and swipes the red stain from his cheek with her fingers. She looks at her hand, young and wrinkle free, sees the sauce on her fingertips and cleans it off with her useful tongue.

Gabriel is dumbstruck and so am I. He needs a girl like this: a classic beauty who, without hesitation, would clean his dirty face with her mouth. A girl like this would keep his mind off of truly messy shit. A girl like this would keep him focused. A girl like this might reinforce the notion that this young man is redeemable, if only due to his ability to attract voluptuous women that inspire my own vicarious fantasies. He could fix his life if he really cared. But he doesn't. He is so lucky but he hasn't got a clue.

I want to help him. I want to say, "Gabriel, go back in the gym and talk to that girl." But we are beyond saying anything that makes sense. My fantasies are his elimination—his disappearance—his farewell letter in which he writes:

Dear Dad,

I'm so sorry for all the trouble I have caused you. I'm leaving now to find myself. I have joined the Merchant Marines and my ship leaves tonight for Singapore. I don't know when I will be back, but when I come home I hope to be the

son and man you can be proud of.
    Love,
    Gabe

Now that makes sense. In Singapore he can meet a nice Singapore girl with a nice Singapore ass and nice Singapore values. Maybe she will be a Buddhist and for once in Gabriel's short life he will find consolation in the spiritual world. I have always liked the Buddhist philosophy. They say, *be open to the possibilities.*

I say, "Damn straight, life is full of them."

"Dad!" he screams. "Drive the fucking car!"

He's back: my mental excursion to the Orient is short-lived. The demon is among us. I turned to look at him and there on his cheek, on the very spot that was once graced by a glob of tomato sauce, is a small barely perceptible stain from my saliva.

"Dad! I have shit to do! I have plans!" he says.

He has plans? I have plans too. Forget the fucking Merchant Marines. How about the United States Marine Corps? There's a plan for you! How do you feel about Iraq, Gabe?

So I move, but not really. I turn on the engine and start to travel. The irony of the car as the antipathy of the exercise machine is not lost on me. My life is a plethora of ironies. I am a walking mass of ironic confusion that enables me to think of everything and nothing, creating my own chaotic peace of mind. In stark physical contrast to the six thousand meters I rowed, the six miles I biked and the three miles I ran without ever moving an inch, I effortlessly traverse the four miles back to my house with barely a physical movement. What does it mean? I don't even know what I'm thinking anymore. The discovery of another piece of irony in my abysmal life is worthless. It is not irony that I seek. I seek the girl with the great ass, the boy on the boat and a wonderful machine that tells me everything I want to hear.

Chapter 11

Hardly a day goes by when I am not confronted by the suffering of others. Everywhere I look I see pain; and what do I do to alleviate the world's suffering? I consciously do nothing, and I know it. And I go to work and I make a good living and I raise a family, and two of my three kids turn out to be really nice. But I always take *it* for granted. What is it? I guess it is life. No! I don't take for granted shit. I just keep moving and never care enough to let the guilt that my mother so tirelessly tried to infuse within me, get to me. So I suppose I understand. Okay, let's say it: I do understand. But this is what happens: I see a man or woman sitting on the sidewalk, sitting on the ground, not in some comfortable beach chair, but sitting on the ground, their asses to the pavement. Their clothes are torn and dirty and they're holding a hat or a cup, or their palms are turned upward. They are begging, they are beggars, but I am always ready with some coins or a dollar to give. I waste more money in a day than most of these people see in a month. So I am ready to give, always ready to cleanse my troubled mind. Occasionally, I am with my boys when I see one of the beggars. When that happens, I tell them to put a dollar in a beggar's cup. And then I instruct either Ethan or Jonathan or Gabriel, depending on which one of them gave the beggar a dollar, to quickly say a prayer for themselves, and beg the Silent and Almighty that they never ever end up as beggars too.

Once I bought a beggar a meal and we had a conversation. He was very dirty but did not appear to be very dangerous. I wanted to say to him, "How did this happen to you?" Or, "Is there something I can do to put you back on your feet?" Or, "Schmuck, get a job! There's a help wanted sign at McDonald's." But I didn't. Instead I said, "Do you think it's going to snow today?" And he said, "I hope not," and we both avoided any real connection to the human level of suffering. So what did I learn? I learned that despite what we are told about hurricanes and typhoons and blizzards and such, that the weather is safe.

And then I'm in London. I'm walking across a bridge that spans the Thames. It's early evening and the city skyline is beginning to light up, reflections of the buildings bouncing off the choppy river. I see the Eye, a circular symbol for a new century, blue and oval from where I stand a few hundred yards away. I see Parliament and Big Ben and the trains moving people across the river against a golden sunset.

There is a man; he is sitting on the ground at the base of the bridge. His hair is cut close to his head and he is wrapped in a blanket that is the color of the Caribbean Sea. He is shivering on a chilly January night. His hat might possibly warm him if he chose to put it on his head, but instead it rests on the ground in front of crossed legs. The hat is brown and woven and sort of a beret with its opening turned up. At its center are a few shiny coins.

My hands are in my pockets as I walk toward him. I can feel the coins that have gathered there along with a few miniature balls of lint, some crumpled paper bills, a pen, a pocket map of London and the train schedule that I picked up at the Marleybone Station. As I approach him I see that he is shaking. His eyes gaze out on the river, perhaps watching the water splashing against the banks. The Thames rises up and down with each passing boat along a great and long expanse of undulating blackness, seemingly flowing in all directions. I wish I knew what he was thinking. Perhaps he was lost in the sadness of his situation. He is expressionless. And then I am nearly in front of him and I know what I should do; I should bring him with me; I should invite him to join me for dinner; I should give him some money. But I keep on walking, my hands stay in my pockets, my coins cold against my fingertips. There have been so many times in so many similar situations when at least I would have offered a token of kindness, but this time, inexplicably, I don't.

I see it all too quickly now, all too late—another test by Him who does not speak to me. And what have I done? I have failed again. I always seem to be failing. I was alone in a foreign city in a distant land and I could have found a companion; I could have extended my hand and done the right thing. But what did I do? Nothing! I am cursed for my inaction! I am reminded of my failure through the voice that resonates between my ears and behind my eyes. It speaks to me although my God does not.

So I carry with me the man in the blue blanket. I wonder what would have happened if I had given him a pound or if I had fed him. He might have told me that he was an angel sent by He who does not speak to me. Maybe he would have said to me, *your worries are over. Your transgressions have been erased and your debts have been forgiven. And your son, remember, your son; you sent him away. He is better and he loves you and he is ready to come home if you are ready to have him.*

The next day I see a woman in the Underground. She is limping as she gets on the train that is crowded with theatergoers heading to the West End of London. Her bag full of clothing, perhaps gifts for her children. As she puts the bag down, the train jerks forward and she falls quickly to the ground. I rush out of my seat to help her, still consumed with the guilt from the night before and the man in the blue blanket. She takes my hand and I help her to her feet and I offer her my seat which she accepts. I look in her eyes, which are mostly brown with tiny specs of yellow, and for an instant I think there is a connection...and I wait...and I wait... and I wait...and then she says, "thank you." But she is not my angel; my angel was the man in the blue blanket—I knew it! Yet again, my failure to recognize a test of He who does not speak to me reinforces my personal sense of doom.

●

Gabriel is my thread. I love him. I hate him. I love him. I hate him. He has brothers. Who are they? They are Ethan and Jonathan. I barely write about them. They are grease; they do not

85

make a sound. They hug me at nighttime before they go to bed, and I am overcome by a delightful feeling of warmth and normalcy. They say to me, "Goodnight, Dad." And I say, "Goodnight, boys." And that's it. It's wonderful.

And then I hear a scream from Paula. It sounds something like this, "Riiiiiiiiiiiiiick!" Yet I'm so used to screaming in my house, that I walk slowly, not urgently, to find out what the problem is. Paula is in the study and it's a mess. Small boxes, black and red and burgundy, are scattered across the floor.

"It can't be happening," she says. "It can't be happening again."

"What are you talking about?" I say.

"My diamond necklace is missing," she replies, pleading as if I might have a clue where it could be.

"What do you mean? Maybe you misplaced it. Maybe one of the boys took it."

She is frantic and on the verge of tears. Twice in the past six months Gabriel has stolen her jewelry. But Gabriel is gone, we sent him away again. He's back where the air is clean and the skies are wide and you sit in the classroom and listen and learn because there's not one other Goddamn thing to do in the entire Goddamn universe. When he left, we stopped worrying about things disappearing. We stopped putting our jewelry in the safe that we purchased to protect our valuables from him.

Then it occurred to me that I also owned a piece of jewelry, a thick gold ring with small diamonds and opals that I purchased on our summer vacation. When Gabriel was home, I never took it off. Now that he was gone, I took it off and put it in the jewelry box with my cheap watches and stainless steel cufflinks. As Paula continued her feverish search through each and every box of real and fake jewelry that she owned, hoping in vain to come across the missing diamond necklace that I had bought her less than two months earlier to replace the one that was stolen by Gabriel, I went into the bedroom to see if my ring was where I left it.

It too was gone. I walked back into the study. Paula was sitting on the floor, still going through her boxes, and I said, "We've been robbed."

And Paula said, "We are cursed." And we are.

He is more than two thousand miles away and he haunts me as much as He who does not speak to me because on a chilly night in London I chose to keep my hands in my pockets.

It had to be one of Gabriel's sleazy friends; there was no doubt about it. There was no forced entry; the thief likely knew the code to the garage door and walked right in. We are idiots to think that we are safe.

Someone just flushed the toilet and the water is running through the pipes. That I hear. That I understand. Hallelujah for bodily functions and the geniuses who designed our sewers. Twice I have hired men to take my son out of my home. The first time there was no more noise than the dirty water running through my pipes. The second time it took three guys with a set of hand-cuffs, the patience of a python, and an absolute belief in He who does not talk to me.

Gabriel wailed and cried and fought like a beaver ready to chew his foot off to get out of a trap. He begged me. "Please, Dad, you promised you wouldn't do this again. You promised," he screamed, as two men held him down on his bed, his voice muffled by the pillow still beneath his head. But what could I do? I couldn't do a thing. I was no longer driven by love; I was driven by the preservation of the remnants of my family. We would survive and we would be safe and we would live without the fear of more destruction. He was seventeen and in nine months would be an adult. In nine months there would be a whole new set of issues confronting Gabriel and us.

For the short-term, however, we were safe. For the short-term I had my flesh and all of the things that ever since I could inhale this earthly breath have shaped my life. The story would continue, of that I was certain. But for the moment, at least, there was a brief respite from everything Gabriel.

Chapter 12

When I was forty I got a job as the Vice President of William Paterson University in Wayne, New Jersey. It was 1997 and Gabriel had just turned seven. My office was in a modestly sized mansion that was the former home of the Vice President of the United States, Garret Hobart, who served one term (before he died) under President William McKinley.

The building was a very cool place. At the beginning of the twentieth century, it was the hub of social high-life in Passaic County, New Jersey. As you entered the building, you were immediately struck by the spiral staircase leading to the second floor which housed a library, a billiard room, a dining room, a social hall with a black baby grand piano and my office with a large marble fireplace. Also on the second floor was a hidden closet that led to a very steep staircase that led to the servants' quarters on the third floor. As the legend goes, the ghost of Garret Hobart's wife resided there.

Hobart Hall was a wonderful place to work, nestled in a quiet corner of the University's hill-top campus. Twenty-four people, including the President of the University, called it their home from nine to five. It was a great place for Gabriel to hang out and explore. Whenever we were there together he was charming and polite. Everyone in the building knew him. They were fond of him and he was fond of them.

Over the years Gabriel became a regular at Hobart Hall. As he got older, he brought his skateboard and rode it around the circular driveway in front of the building. A slight hill led into the driveway and I often saw him from my window, coming down the hill, his arms outstretched for balance, as he glided to the front door and ran up the stairs to my office. Had it been a University student riding a skateboard in front of the President's office, the campus police would surely have been called, but Gabriel was so much a fixture and so liked that everyone just let it go.

I loved taking him to work. I loved showing him off. I loved that my colleagues could see how smart he was. Once, when he was ten, he wanted to explore the third floor, which had not been renovated like the rest of the building. Afraid of what he might find, he approached one of my colleagues and asked him if he had ever been to the third floor.

Gabriel said, "Why don't we go up there together and I can show you around." To which my colleague replied, "That sounds like a great idea, I've never been up there," knowing full well that he was being tricked by Gabriel to provide an adult escort into the haunted areas of Hobart Hall.

By the time he was thirteen, coming to campus had lost its thrill. His pre-adolescent machismo was beginning to take shape. Yet when I told him that I was leaving the University for another job, he began to cry, perhaps recognizing that one phase of his life was over and another, far less innocent, was about to begin.

•

Let me tell you about my wife. She is pretty, she is smart, and she is gliding ever so gracefully toward the unfathomable age of fifty. Twenty-four years ago, when we first began our less than perfect journey together as husband and wife, she would often ask me why I chose to marry her. It seemed an odd question for a new bride to be asking her new husband, but then again we were and are one of those opposite poles couples. You know the kind: she is the Ying—I am the Yang. The strength of our marriage and friendship were those things for which we complemented each other, not necessarily the things we had in common. I, of course, was a little rough around the edges. And, she, naturally, was a bit more genteel and refined. There was also the whole love thing, the indefinable bits of magic and scents and allure which centuries of philosophers have yet to finger precisely. So why did I marry Paula? The truth is that there were many non-sexual, non-love, long-term and pragmatic issues that I, as a twenty-eight-year-old man fast-tracking his career with the Boy Scouts of America, felt compelled to address. What she had, what I coveted most in her being, were those practical qualities entirely foreign to my DNA. The pretty piece was good, but the smart piece was better. I had absolutely no faith in my personal gene pool. I had never considered myself to be much of a thinker. Yet if I was ever to breed, I felt compelled to pass on a genetic code that highly improved upon my own.

In addition to her intellect, I must say that I greatly admired Paula's discipline. She had gone from high school to college to graduate school to completing her Ph.D. without ever taking a break to get high or drunk or laid by some guy whom she gladly forgot before filling her bowl with cereal the next morning. Early in our courtship, I often caught her studying, reading and doing academic research. What the hell was that about? These were wholly foreign notions to my educational experience. My education consisted of the slippery path of least resistance in which the slightest amount of attention to the smallest amount of detail miraculously sufficed to get me in and out of college. So I said to myself, *this is a woman I could breed with*. This is a woman who would not bore me. This is a woman whom I could trick with my bad poetry and faux love of nature. And she would see that in twenty years I might be interesting, too ... maybe.

So we wed. A beautiful day...a blushing bride...a proud Mama and Papa...a hint of hyacinth in the air as I smashed the glass and kissed the bride and dreamed of unlimited sex and little babies and baseball games and love.

Several years later we tried to make a family. Unfortunately, it didn't go as planned. Then we adopted our magnificent son, Gabriel. And then—wonder of wonder, miracle of miracles—Paula gave birth to Ethan and Jonathan, and all of a sudden we were a family of five. But happiness continued to be an elusive bastard. Gabriel, the prophet, the angel, the illumination of our lives, had begun to transform into something dark, unreasonable and unmanageable.

By the time he was fourteen, we had completely lost control. Our lives became a nightmare of fighting and cursing and where is he now and what has he done and how could a God that loves anyone (including us) do this to two kind and wonderful people, such as we were.

So my wonderful wife, my brilliant wife, my—dare I say—soul mate, had an epiphany. She had come to the actualization that we were the problem. That if we were fixed, then the nightmare that we lovingly called Gabriel would follow suit. How, you might ask, did a woman of her intellect arrive at this breakthrough revelation? Was she choking on an olive when it came to her? Was she blow-drying her hair, imagining herself on a secluded beach, naked and uninhibited, when a swarthy young buckaroo approached her and said, "It's you." Or did she see these words early one morning, floating in her organic milk and Alphabets cereal. The letters, shifting as if a higher power, a deity that spoke to her but not to me, were sending her a message. And it was those two words, again and again and again, "It's you. It's you. It's you." And despite her frantic attempts to eat the words, despite the chewing and the mouthfuls of cold cereal, and the crunching of i's and t's and o's and u's, the words continued to emerge from the depths of her milky bowl, rising to the white rippling surface. "It's you."

If only our lives were driven by such imagery then perhaps we could better appreciate the awful gestalt of our being. It would have been good to know that there was a magical presence guiding us, leading us, even torturing us. But no, our lives were driven by a randomness that was less than the wind but more than a sneeze.

Paula's revelation was a combination of practicality and desperation. Her Ph.D. and her gut and her license in clinical psychology led her to put her faith in a man she had just met. She was attending a conference that had something to do with a variety of modalities for treating aberrant youth. Of course, the first thing that came to my mind when I heard about the conference was that I should be leading it. Was I not the father of the Emperor of youthful aberrant behavior? Knives, drugs, booze and sex were four words that aptly described what I was living through with Gabriel. Yet the conference organizers had other ideas. They wanted presenters who had successfully dealt with aberrant children, not just experienced them. They had no interest in a suffering father who wrote pithy vignettes about the ultimate destruction of his son.

One of the presenters at the conference was a man named Dr. Maurice West, who very much impressed Dr. Paula Kaplan-Reiss, who wanted nothing else in the universe than to help and understand the wayward boy, Gabriel. What can I say about Dr. West? He was big. He was black. He was adopted. I think he was a cowboy. He had a theory about fucked-up kids. He said that trauma begets trauma and that traumatized parents unwittingly traumatize their children through often indiscernible acts, including acts of kindness, but mostly acts of neglect and misunderstanding. The blame, therefore, was really on the grandparents or great-grandparents or even great-great-grandparents, who traumatized their children who traumatized their children who then (big surprise) traumatize their children, too. They were the parents who swallowed the dog to catch the cat, who swallowed the mouse to catch the spider that wiggled and jiggled and tickled inside her. They swallowed the spider to catch the fly, they swallowed the fly, I don't know why—I wish I knew why they swallowed the fly...perhaps to die?

How ironic then, that many of these fly and spider eating parents had been traumatized by the actions of their children, actions that they unknowingly caused as a result of their own trauma at the hands of their own parents who no doubt were traumatized by their own parents generations ago. And the poor violent child, what is his or her fate? They hated Mom and Dad. They hated us (me and Paula to be specific) because, in our case, we never got over our infertility. And since we never got over our infertility, (even though we had two biological children) we never accepted our adopted son. This, on top of seventeen generations of trauma, had made us the worst parents since Genghis Khan, who, as I am sure you know, ate his children. Yet there was hope. According to Dr. West, these acts of violence and anger can and would stop once we, the parents, understood our own trauma brought upon by our parents (or others) who were of course traumatized by their parents (or others) going all the way back to the days of Jesus on the cross. Dr. West said that 99.9 percent of all traumas resulted in fear and caused anger, and that 99.9 percent of this was passed from one generation to the next.

Now comes the good part; he was coming to my house. He was coming to my house with his dreadlocks and his western ease and his sympathetic face and his kick-ass cowboy boots for a three-day all-expense paid romp through our subconscious minds. Praise the Lord! And praise the most important God of all: the American dollar. Can you say $6,000? Say it again like you mean it. Say it to He who does not speak to me, but might be speaking to her. Say it to the bank that just approved my loan. That's six thousand naked buckaroos in the sunshine of Dr. West's wallet.

What can I say? An epiphany knows no boundaries. He was coming all the way from Colorado to New Jersey. Giddy-up.

●

Dr. West was in my house. He was sitting on my patio reading a book about marketing that I gave him. I asked him if he liked the book. He said it's pretty good and went on to tell me how someday he hopes to franchise his therapeutic centers. He didn't say so, but I can tell from the way he talked, imbued with a confident nonchalance, that he would like to be the king of family therapy. Wendy's. McDonald's. Burger King. Therapy King. *I'd like a little detachment therapy today. Hold the Freudian slips.*

We planned to begin our first session as soon as the kids left for school. I began by asking Dr. West a question.

"How old are you?" I asked.

"How old do you think I am?" he responded. In my head I was thinking he was thirty-something. But that wasn't the point, was it: how about a straight answer?

I asked him another question: "Do you have children?"

He paused for a moment, turned his head to the east, absorbing the warmth of a rising sun, and said, "Do you think it's important

93

that I have children?"

I wanted to kill him. We hadn't even begun but already I was having a visceral reaction to this congenial fellow. What did I know about him? He was from Colorado where the mountains are really big and there are lots of them. He was adopted and so I had a predilection toward him regardless of the $6,000 I was shelling out. He seemed very laid-back, perhaps too laid-back given the magnitude of our predicament. Yet I wondered if someone was protecting him too. Perhaps his adoptive parents were of the Lakota people of Western Colorado. The ancient Lakotas believed in the legend of the White Buffalo. The birth of the White Buffalo calf signified the coming together of humanity into a oneness of heart, mind and spirit. Was Dr. West my Black Buffalo, bringing oneness to my family? Did the White Buffalo protect him? The question was beyond rhetorical. There were no buffalos. It was only He who does not speak to me watching over Dr. West.

Gabriel spoke to me that morning before he left for school. He said, "What the fuck is he doing here?"

I said, "He is for us, not you. Go away."

"I hate him," said Gabriel.

We began. The first thing we did was remove a large coffee table from the living room and take it into the dining room. That created a large open space on the floor. Next we removed the cushions from the two matching sofas and placed them in the space formerly occupied by the coffee table.

Dr. West said, "Paula and Rick, I want you to lie next to each other on the cushions.

We lay down.

"Now, I want you to roll on your sides and face each other."

We rolled to our sides, Paula to her left and me to my right. "Now, I want you to close your eyes and embrace." We closed our eyes and embraced. He said, "Rick, do you feel safe in Paula's arms?"

"Yes," I answered.

"Paula, do you feel safe in Rick's arms?"

"Yes," she said.

And then I heard a noise. It was a miniature gong that Dr. West brought with him to begin our session. He struck it three times with a small cotton covered mallet and said, "Paula and Rick, the ancient Tibetans...

(Okay, all I can say was that it was so hard, I mean really really super really hard for me to, A) not laugh uncontrollably, and B) not stand up and slap Dr. Black Buffalo Man From Colorado and his Tibetan gong. Not that I had anything against cowboys. Who didn't want to be a cowboy? I had a cap-gun pistol and a holster and when I was six years old I was prepared to shoot any and all Injuns that made their way to Pompton Plains, New Jersey. And I had nothing against the good people of Colorado, a picturesque state where I have vacationed. And I especially had nothing against psychologists. I married one for crying out loud! But a gong? In my house? On my floor?)... believed that upon hearing the sounding of the gong one's mind opened to new possibilities. Rick, are you open?"

"Yes," I said, trying my best to maintain the solemnity of the moment.

"Paula," he said, "Are you open?"

Nothing. "Paula," he said again. "Are you open?" Still nothing.

I opened my eyes and looked at Paula. There was a tear trickling down the side of her face. Her cheeks were bright red.

"Paula," he implored for a third time. "Are you open?"

"Yes," she blurted out. "Yes, of course," she spewed, as her entire body shook. "Yes! Yes! Yes!" she said laughing uncontrollably, quivering in my arms, tears pouring out of her eyes, flowing like the mighty Colorado River, which a millennium ago was the source of all life to the ancestors of the adoptive parents of Dr. Colorado Cowboy and his Buddhist cousins.

"Yes! Of Course!" she said, still laughing, still shaking in my embrace.

And then she stopped and was calm. It was an instant transformation, as if someone or something or He who speaks to her but not to me, slapped her on the ass and said, knock it off, it was your idea to hire this guy! Her face was serene and tranquil. She was caught in a zephyr, floating away to a place where life was sweet. She closed her eyes and relaxed her body and pressed her moist tear-stained cheek to mine.

I wanted to go with her, but first I wanted to laugh like she had just done, deep and loud and guttural, acknowledging not only how ludicrous this was, but how perverse too. What in the world was Black Buffalo Adopted Buddhist Man and his Ph.D. doing in my house?

Here we go."Rick," he said, "We're going to start with you. I want you to think back. Think back to your earliest memories. What do you remember?"

This was easy; I had done this before. I had this conversation with friends and siblings and even my parents. I said, "I remember that when I was two we went to Florida by train. I remember seeing a man wrestle an alligator. I remember the glass bottom boats. I remember the train broke down and the passengers, including me, got off the train."

And then I felt something against me. There was a pressure on my body and I realized that Dr. West was kneeling beside me and leaning into me. His hands were pressing against my back, not in a gentle way but as if he were supporting his own weight against my body. He was heavy. He was a big man. He looked like a fullback and if his arms were to suddenly give out from under him, the force of his body falling on mine would surely cause me harm.

"Rick," he said, "do you feel safe?

"Yes," I answered, "I feel fine," although clearly my breathing had become heavier as a result of his body leaning into mine. "It sounds like a nice family trip," he said.

"I think it was," I answered.

"Let's move forward. Was there anything about your childhood that bothered you?"

Wow! Did I really want to do this? Did I really want to go there? Did Dr. Black Buffalo Cowboy Adopted Buddhist Fullback with or without children need to know this? And where would it take me? Perhaps someplace dark or hidden—a repressed memory that when actualized would open a vista of possibilities, freeing me from the burden of my miserable past and enabling me to create a new life of blissful contentment. Why not? I had already paid the son-of-a-bitch.

"I was picked on," I said. "You were picked on?" he repeated a bit joyfully, like he has just realized how wonderful it is to catch a snowflake on your tongue. "Why did people pick on you?"

"I was fat. I got picked on a lot," I said. Paula said nothing. Her job was to hold me tight and keep me safe through the sad journey of my life. He leaned into me more. I think Paula was giggling, but I kept my eyes closed, determined to see where all this is going.

"That must have hurt," said Dr. West. "Who picked on you?"

"Everyone," I said. "Everyone picked on me. Bullies picked on me and beat me up. My father made fun of me because I was fat. And the gym teacher was always riding me. Once he slammed me into a locker because I couldn't do a push-up."

And then, I don't know why, maybe it was the safety of being in Paula's arms. Maybe it was the weight of Fullback Cowboy Buddhist Shrink, or maybe, like the Grinch, my heart opened up and all the little Who's in Whoville filled my very being with joy. But whatever the reason between me and Paula, or me and Dr. West, or me and the fella or feller that sends messages to my wife via her cereal but never to me, I just let go. And for no particular reason, other than the obvious sadness of my wretched life, I slowly but surely began to weep like a baby. Paula squeezed a little tighter. Dr. West pushed a little harder. He asked me, "What did you want?"

"I don't know," I said. "Come on, Rick. What did you want?" he asked again. "I really don't know," I repeated. "Yes, you do," he said in a commanding voice. "Now tell me. What did you want?"

"I wanted them to stop. I wanted them to go away. Why were they doing this? I never did anything to anybody," I said, as the tears poured from my eyes and my voice trembled, choking on the gargantuan lump that was forming in my throat.

"Why do you think they picked on you," he pressed on.

"I really don't know. It was horrible," I said, as tiny salt-water puddles gathered in the places where my cheek pressed hard against

Paula's face.

"Why didn't you fight back?" he asked.

"I was too afraid," I said. "I think I'm still afraid."

"If you were there today," said Dr. West, "what would you say to them?"

By then the words were hard to bring out. I was drenched in sweat and tears and the heat of the two bodies surrounding me. Paula was clinging to me and Dr. West was on me like a cat that has just pounced on a big fat rat.

"Stop it!" I shouted. "Just go away! Leave!...Me!...Alone! Why can't you just leave me alone?"

And they did. I felt Dr. West pulling away. Sensitive Dreadlock Buddhist Buffalo Doctor Fullback Therapy King was gently easing off me as my breathing returned to normal. I open my tear-filled eyes and looked at Paula. She eased her clasp around me.

"Are you okay?" I asked.

"I'm okay," she said, sounding a bit confused. "How are you?"

"I'm great," I said. "That was a little weird."

As I rolled to my back and sat up, there was the King of all Therapy still sitting beside me, smiling slightly, with a bit of a smug I-told-you-so look on his face. I knew what he was thinking: Ka-Ching! No refund here. But wait! What's that? He was crying too. Give me a fucking break! He must have thought I was a cold heartless bastard who turned his boy into a beast. He must have thought he would never break through the icy façade that is the dark aura that surrounds me. Yet he did, and he joined me in my sadness, my revelation, my coming to grips with all those years of being bullied. I guess it was supposed to make me feel good that he cried with me, but I think I resented that too.So, okay, I was tortured as a child. So what? It's not like this was some huge hidden secret that I never dealt with. I did deal with it. I grew up. I moved on. I got old. Was this the source of Gabriel's anger? Come on. There had to be something else, something innate, a disconnect that we had yet to put a handle on. This theory of his was too simplistic, and the fact that on top of everything else, Dr. West turned out to be the Barbara Walters of family therapy did little to convince me of the value of my personal cry-fest with or without the tumultuous Colorado flowing from his eye sockets.

In the end, I drove Barbara Blackman Rastafarian back to the airport. We did a couple of more sessions, minus the tears, in which no great revelations came forth. For Paula, it was so much more than merely disappointing. In three short days she learned to despise Dr. West. She never bought into the whole lean-on-me process, and in fact, when he asked her during therapy how she felt as he pressed against her, she said that she felt like there was an anvil on her back. A deep thinker might say the anvil was Gabriel, but surprisingly the blacksmith and his anvil and his lasso and Ph.D. and his middle journey from the Gold Coast of Africa to the snow covered peaks of the Colorado Rockies never took us there, not once. The anvil was Dr. West, and the hammer would still torture us no matter what we did or didn't know about our own personal traumas and those of our ancestors. Sparks were a-comin'. Oh, Lord, they were a-comin'.

Chapter 13

No more hugs and kisses for Gabriel. Not here. Not ever. No way in the miserable universe of being will I ever return to being that sap, that forlorn yet empathic father: caring—loving—concerned. Hate is easy. Hate is simple. Hate is me. It's savage. It's sad. It's all of these things because what I have discovered is that everything is grist for the mill. Not that I really know what a grist mill is. I've been told that it has something to do with wheat and flour and millstones. Look up millstone for yourself, but if you know what grist is, you'll likely know what a millstone is, too. From what I have gathered, all this grist gets ground up in the millstone and out comes a soft powder that is not anthrax although it may look like anthrax. But it's flour. It makes bread. It is the sustenance of life. Everything is grist. I grind it up in my mind and out comes a story that is partially or mostly or wholly true. Yet for me, the truth was simply too unbearable to accept. Every expression of compassion was met with another punch in the eye. The story never ended; it only got worse. One more threat, one more lie, one more interruption in my quest for a normal family.

Truth is a bitch! It sucks. It hurts. It interrupts everything important.

●

Lunch was over. I paid the bill, debating with Paula over the size of the tip (she said more, I said less). As we walked out the door I noticed a large oval bowl next to the cash register filled with hundreds of pieces of colorful hard candy. There were red and white striped peppermints and brown root beers that were neatly wrapped in clear cellophane. And there were lots of jelly-filled hard candies, the color of a grey ocean, that were the mainstay of my grandmother's living room in her apartment in the Bronx overlooking the railroad tracks where we would wait like children (oh right, we were children) for the trains to go speeding by as the entire building shook. Ordinarily, and for sheer nostalgic pleasure, I would have chosen the hard candy filled with strawberry or cherry or lemon filling. But the anchovies in my Caesar Salad, not to mention the seven pounds of garlic in the shrimp scampi I just consumed, created an unpleasant oral sensation that not only affected me, but also had the power to affect those within breathing distance. Therefore, I chose a circular peppermint that was as thick as my thumb and about the size of a quarter in diameter.

Back inside the car, seatbelt securely fastened, I plopped the candy into my mouth. I swirled it around for a few seconds, moving it from the right side of my mouth to the left, as slowly its minty flavor overcame the disagreeable aftertaste of garlic and anchovy. And then I did what I always do when eating a piece of hard candy. I chomped on it like a hammer coming down on a walnut. Tiny shards of sugar exploded in my mouth, sharp and piercing against my flesh, but lacking the force to do damage as I experienced a sudden burst of flavor traveling from the former confines of the hard candy shell—the very shell that previously occupied a small corner of my mouth—to every region of that bodily orifice that is the home to thirty-two yellow-stained teeth. I swirled the candy shrapnel in my mouth, continuing to chew, as it quickly dissolved along with its refreshing flavor.

Paula was aghast. After nearly twenty-three years of marriage she had yet to come to grips with my need for immediate gratification, including, but not limited to, my habit of crushing hard candy.

"Don't you *want* it to last?" she asked me, her voice tinged with derision.

"It does last," I cheerfully replied.

"Yeah, thirty seconds," she said. "When I put a mint in my mouth, I never bite it. And do you know why? I never bite it because you're supposed to suck on them. You don't know how to suck," she stated with outlandish pride.

"I do, too," I said. "I just prefer not to. I can suck as good as anyone."

"I don't think so," she said. "In fact, you know what I think? I think if you were a woman... or if you were gay... you could never give a decent blowjob. You would put some guy's penis in your mouth, swirl it around for a few seconds, and bite its head off."

"I disagree," I said rather indignantly. "I can suck as long as anyone. And I'll tell you something else. You find me the man. You bring him here. And I am on it. You understand what I'm saying?"

"Really," she said in a superior tone, confident in her understanding of my masculine impulsivity.

"Yeah. Really," I answered. "Do you want to watch? Do you need empirical evidence since obviously my word is not enough?"

And then she did something remarkable. She opened her purse and took out a small blue and silver tin filled with breath mints. The mints were smaller than the one I had taken from the restaurant, about the size of a penny. Still smiling, she put one in her mouth, balancing it delicately on her tongue before placing it between her upper and lower front teeth. Then, like a great white vice, she forced her teeth together smashing the mint in the process. As she continued to chew, I could hear what remained of the candy being crushed in her mouth.

She is a devil! This woman plays me. Just when I think I can take her no more, she tricks me with a shared sexual ambivalence that is intimately close to my own misunderstanding of self. In a horrible way, it's delightful. I love her and I hate her—love (and lust) being the operative theme of the moment.

It would have been wonderful to consummate our ambivalence at that very instant. What a pleasure it would have been to share a few more mints and a bit more sucking. Even a kiss, minty fresh, would have been delightful. Yet as soon as we got home and walked through the door, reality struck, as it often did, slowly at first, then building to its inevitable conclusion of massive force.

Paula, of course, is laughing uncontrollably. Her laugh is deep and rich and filled with a heartiness that is emblematic of a life well lived despite our shared troubles. She is sitting on a rose colored sofa in our living room. The sofa is soft, worn leather. She is wearing a tight-fitting shirt with large floral prints. I am hardly a fan of prints of any kind, but I am willing to ignore her questionable taste in what amounts to no more than a second layer of skin. It's what's under the florals that draws me to her. It's the mental game she's begun. She has joined me in my weakness, my inability to suck, and is totally amused by her trickery. I watched her as she crossed her legs, as she smiled, as she reached for a magazine that she may or may not have wanted to read.

She looked good and I wanted her. I rose from where I sat, my own rose-colored sofa, identical and parallel to hers, and planned to take her, mint and all. I checked my watch—thirty minutes until the boys would be home from school. It's nice to think that after twenty-five years there is still a bit of hunt left in me. I eyed my prey. I hopped from sofa to sofa and handed her a second mint that I took from the restaurant. I said, "Care for a bite?"

She laughed again and I smiled. I took her hand and put it to my lips, sliding her index finger across my tongue. I checked my watch again—twenty five minutes until the kids are home. Let's see who sucks the best. With her moist hand in mine, we began to walk toward the bedroom. And then—perfectly—justly—because why should I have any more joy than my pathetic fantasies would allow, the doorbell rang.

On this day, my mouth fresh with mint and desire, my heart smothered in garlic and anchovies, and my hand encasing a warm wet finger, I realized yet again how painfully unlucky I was. Standing at my door was a man in a uniform. He was not a policeman but he was an employee of the United States government. He was my mailman and he had several items for me, none of which, thankfully, were an anthrax filled envelope. He had a postcard from a lovely Jersey Shore B&B that Paula and I stayed at several years ago. The postcard asked us to stay once more for a romantic winter weekend. He had the phone bill and the most recent issue of *Better Homes and*

Gardens, and notification from a bank I never heard of that informed me that I had been pre-approved for a new credit card with $35,000 limit and 1.9% APR for any transfers I make to the new card from any or all of my old cards as long as I paid everything off within eighteen months. And he had a large green envelope that I had to sign for. I recognized the dot matrix print on the outside. It was a summons from the Middlesex County Juvenile Court. They were looking for Gabriel but they would not find him. They had their chance and they blew it. They would have to settle for me.

The judge will not be pleased when she finds out that we sent Gabriel away; she wants him back. The judge will be mad, really mad, because without her permission I shipped him out. I took away the Court's prerogative to incarcerate him. How did this make me feel? Let me think a moment. Moment over…fuck the court! I begged the court to place him in a residential treatment center and the court refused. I had overwhelming evidence against my son but it seemed not to matter, the judge was sending him home. When the horror of her decision sank in, this is what I said—no, this is what I yelled to the judge as Paula sat beside me crying: "You should be ashamed of yourself! You have no idea what you're doing!"

Now, that's a memory, a story, a great gob of grist for the giant millstone of life.

And that was that. So much for sex. So much for moist fingers and minty breaths, and anchovies and garlic and a hint of passion and a spring in my step. As soon as the mailman arrived, any hope for a conjugal visit flew out the window with the Pony Express. Mint notwithstanding, the law has a sobering effect on sexual organs, especially when the sexual organ in question is the brain. And receiving a summons, well, what can I say? It is a wholly unpleasant experience. It sucks along with my life, and if I could crush it and swallow it I would. Let's back it up. Here we go—more truth.

●

Gabriel is running. By the time he is seventeen he is really fast, so I don't bother chasing him anymore. I suppose I could run him down tortoise-like, but doing so would imply that I cared. I didn't. He is burying himself, at least that's what I thought and what I hoped. I picked up the phone instead and called the police. I informed them that my son, who was already under house arrest, had left the house. No need for details. No need to fill them in on why. Why was irrelevant. The police would come to the house. They would make a report. They would file the report with Gabriel's probation officer. The probation officer would be forced to file a complaint with the Juvenile Court, and the Juvenile Court would issue a summons for Gabriel to appear. Although I didn't know it at the time, it was the beginning of the end for Gabriel: my sucky life turning into his sucky life—all of it leading to an early morning abduction of my son. This would be Gabriel's second abduction in three years...a nightmare for him, a blessed reprieve for me.

●

Black clouds and thunder filled the skies that morning as we awoke to make our first court appearance in nearly two years. Crows were circling over our house. Dead frogs covered our driveway and there was a scent of sulfur in the air. If only it were true; if only there was a dark omniscient foreshadowing to give us hope. Wouldn't that have been lovely? In truth, it was sunny and cool, a good day to go ice skating, but apparently not a good day to beg for the incarceration of a seventeen-year-old boy. The act that brought us to court (breaking house arrest) was nothing compared to Gabriel's more recent extracurricular activities. He was simply out of control and we realized that allowing him to live in our home was no longer viable. The sad truth (again) is that he stole a diamond necklace and diamond earrings from Paula. He stole money from his brothers. He hardly went to school. And he had become increasingly violent and abusive toward Paula and me. During one incident he threw a telephone at Paula. During another incident he punched me. During another incident he put his fist through the dining room wall. Or he walked around the house brandishing a steak knife. Or he was swinging a golf club. Or he was high. Or he was drunk, a lit cigarette dangling from his lips like a silent fuck you to Mom and Dad.

Our plan was to beg the court to help us get him out of our home. Surely, there were state-run programs for boys like him. It was all too obvious how bad our situation had become. How could any reasonable person not see that and want to help?

The courtroom was not so large, about the size of a small restaurant. The Judge was the Maitre d', perched high on her bench, controlling the flow of activity. The prosecutors were the captains. The clerks were the wait staff. The police were the dishwashers, dutifully attending to all the dirty work. And we were customers hoping for a decent meal.

"Gabriel," asked the judge, "Why are you here? I see you violated house arrest. Why would you do that?"

"My Dad and I were fighting," he said. "So I took off."

"Do you do that a lot," asked the Judge. "Fight with your Dad?"

"We just don't get along," said Gabriel calmly.

"Why do you think that is?" she begged on.

"I don't know," he said. "It seems like we're always fighting."

"And what about your Mom? Do you get along with her?"

"Not at all," answered Gabriel a bit more stoically.

He was calm under duress. He knew she could lock him up in the blink of an eye and he never blinked once. He was in his most wonderful sociopathic smart young man mode. He looked good. He stood erect. He lied with the ease of a morning glory that opens automatically to the sun's first rays, oblivious of any conscious effort to spread its petals.

"Gabriel," the judge said once again in a sympathetic voice, "you're seventeen. What are your plans?"

I could see it coming. I heard the bullshit so many times and he delivers it so well.

"First, I want to finish high school," he said. "Then I want to go to the community college to learn how to be a mechanic. Then I want to go to Rutgers to get a degree in business so I can start my own car repair shop."

"I'd like to hear from the prosecutor now," said the Judge.

The prosecutor was a young man who was probably twenty-eight, but looked more like eighteen. Among the things he never learned in law school was how to dress. He wore a black sportcoat, an orange shirt and a blue tie. Perhaps he thought he was a tiger lily? He said, "Your Honor, this is a very minor infraction and we see no cause to incarcerate Mr. Reiss. In fact, I find him to be one of the most articulate young men to come before the Court in a very long time."

Just shoot me now. Please. I counted at least four policemen in the room, none of whom had a tray of dirty dishes and all of whom have a spiffy little gun strapped to their hips. What would it take to get shot? I could lurch for the Judge; that might work. But she hasn't fully enraged me yet.

"I'd like to hear from the parents now," she said.

And so it was my turn. I stood slowly, prepared to betray my son. I was optimistic that the judge would hear my plea and help us. I accepted that the prosecutor was too young and inexperienced to recognize that Gabriel was saying what they expected him to say. He was right about one thing, though. Gabriel is smart, too smart. The Judge would see this, I was sure.

I was polite at first. I said, "Your honor. Gabriel hasn't been to school in two weeks. He stays up all night and sleeps all day. We believe he has stolen some very valuable jewelry from us. Two days ago, he took a blank check out of my check book and tried to cash it at a local bank. When the bank asked him for I.D., he fled. But it's worse, much worse. He regularly threatens me, my wife and my children. He curses at us all the time. He throws things at us. He frightens his brothers. He terrorizes our family. He thinks he can do anything, and he does. We live in an unlivable situation. Just the other day, he was walking around with a steak knife and threw it into the dining room wall. I was on a business trip in Florida last week and he called me during a meeting and told me he was going to smash my wife's head in with a brick. Here is the message he left me on my cell phone."

I flipped open my cell phone, pressed a few buttons and put it on speaker. It's Gabriel's voice: *Dad, you fucking piece of shit. I fucking hate you and I'm going to kill you and mom.*

"You need to help us," I begged her. "You need to take him out of our home. My home is not safe for my family. I know this is not the reason we're here," I went on, "but we need help. We can't continue to live our lives in fear."

"Gabriel, is what your father saying true?" she asked him. "Why aren't you going to school?"

School? What the hell is she talking about? Did she blackout while I was speaking? Did she have one of those mini strokes when I played the recording?

A waiter nudged Gabriel to stand while the Judge spoke to him.

"I have trouble sleeping," he said, "but I did go to school this week."

That was true. In the last three weeks, Gabriel had been to school four times, including the two days preceding our appearance in court.

"When you come home from school, do you do your homework?"

"I don't get homework in my school."

"So what do you do when you get home?"

"I usually go to my best friend's house."

"What does your room look like?"

"It's very messy."

"Do you clean your room?"

"No."

"Why not?"

"I just don't."

"What about drugs."

"I don't do drugs."

"If I gave you a urine test right now, would you fail?"

"Possibly."

"So you are using drugs."

"Just pot."

"Gabriel. Sit down," said the Judge.

He sat dutifully like an obedient puppy. He was a model sociopath. He listened to the judge because she is not his mother. His mother can't put him in jail. When the judge spoke, Gabriel was focused. He was an unwavering bullet on a path aimed at my skull. Not even a mighty wind could take him off course. For the moment, however, the judge was the power and Gabriel knew it.

I wanted to ask her to come and live with us. Her presence could have been just the thing to improve Gabriel's behavior. I should have asked her if she likes milk or sugar or both with her morning tea. It would have been delightful to have her at the breakfast table. I'm sure Gabriel would have been thrilled as well. Not that he is ever up for breakfast.

She spoke: "First, as for the offense, I am extending Gabriel's probation for another six months. I am also ordering that Gabriel get drug counseling. I am also ordering that Gabriel attend a weekly Narcotics Anonymous group. I don't know the Reiss family, but it seems to me that there is a real communication problem. I am ordering that Gabriel and Mr. and Mrs. Reiss undergo psychiatric evaluations. They all need family counseling. And one more thing. Gabriel, stand up."

"Gabriel, when you get home from school every day I am ordering you to clean your room," she said with the solemnity of a real judge ordering a real sentence.

Holy shit, I thought to myself. Please...Jesus, Moses, Mother Mary come to me...can she really be this stupid?

I looked to my left where Paula was sitting. She was crying. She knew we were sunk. What kind of a jack-ass of a judge orders a seventeen-year-old boy to clean his room every day as punishment for threatening to kill his parents on a regular basis?

I looked around the courtroom. The waiters and dishwashers were shaking their collective heads. They couldn't believe that they were required to serve this crap.

My hand was forced. If I said nothing, I was emasculated. I

had to respond. I had to show He who does not speak to me that within this creature that He may or may not have created that there exists the integrity to right this abominable wrong.

Without asking or being asked I stood again. "Your honor," I said with force and determination, unable to accept the judge's ruling. "You have no idea what you're doing. You are putting my family at risk. Do you understand that?" I shouted. "This isn't right!"

She said nothing, she didn't have to. I had smashed court protocol as quickly as I had smashed a cool mint in my mouth. Cliché be damned, but if looks could kill, I was dead where I stood.

And then I said, "You should be ashamed of yourself. Shame on you! Shame on you! You don't know what you've done!"

"Mr. Reiss," she said, and that was enough. Every eye in the courtroom was on me. Some were empathic and some were bewildered, but all of them knew I had better shut-up and shut-up fast. Right or wrong she was still the judge and I was totally, absolutely, and perhaps eternally screwed.

I hated this bitch nearly as much as I hated Gabriel at that moment. She was as clueless as he.

She said, "I will see all of you again in forty-five days for a progress report and you'd better be courteous."

So we left, Gabriel quietly laughing, telling Paula that we were the crazy ones and that the judge and everyone else knew that, too. He was the boss now, empowered like he had never been before. I had tried to protect us and society from this fanatical, violent, adolescent boy, but lost big time. Game over. He won.

Even He who does not speak to me might not have seen how bad our lives were about to become. Within ten days of Gabriel's court appearance he would be handcuffed in his room by three men that we paid six thousand dollars to take him to a lock-down therapeutic boarding school in Utah. It took them two hours to get him out of our house and twenty-four hours to get him to Utah, including a twelve-hour drive from New Jersey to Chicago to give Gabriel some time to calm down in order to put him on a plane and take off the handcuffs.

So here is the big surprise and the outcome of the judge's ruling. Not once did Gabriel clean his room. Within a week he was permanently thrown out of school. Within twenty-four hours the police were at our house because Gabriel was threatening us. (He wanted money. We said no.) Within seventy-two hours the police were back. (He wanted money. We said no again.) This time, when Gabriel saw the police cars pulling up to our house, he took off. As he ran out the back door he dropped the hammer and the twelve-inch screwdriver that he had been using to break into our safe. Remarkably, he returned a half an hour later, while the police were still in our home. I am sure he thought that once again nothing would happen, but this time the police cuffed him.

"No, no, no, no." Gabriel said, surprised and angry. "What the fuck are you doing?"

"Gabe," said the policeman, "Calm down."

"I can't go back," he wailed, understanding fully what was about to happen. "You don't understand. I will fucking kill myself. I promise." And he began to bang his head fiercely against the wall, several strands of his wonderful henna-colored hair sticking to a small crack in the molding. He kicked like a wild man, still yelling, "No! No! No!" And Paula and I and Ethan and Jonathan said not a word as we calmly watched him disintegrate. The police took quick action as the head banging intensified and quickly dropped Gabriel to the floor. His hands behind his back—his face pressed into the hallway runner—his body held in place by an officer's knee strategically positioned in the middle of his back.

Gabriel's performance kept him out of the Juvenile Detention Center. Instead, the police sent him to an adolescent psychiatric ward where all the geniuses with all their Ph.D.s and MDs and Master of Social Work degrees, determined that his problems were behavioral not psychological. I pleaded with them to keep Gabriel until I could make other arrangements. But they had no interest in giving up a taxpayer supported bed for my lunatic of a son. I would have to take him home...feed him...clothe him...fear him. So I closed my eyes for a moment and revived my faith in the Invisible

One who does not speak to me. I never questioned why; I only asked for help. But what I got was the same as always. Silence.

When I opened my eyes, I saw before me a tired young man. At three in the morning Gabriel could be quite reasonable. His eyes were red and his wrists were sore and slightly swollen from the handcuffs the police had put on him when they took him from our house. He was seventeen and I had seen him in handcuffs four times in his life. Not a life for anyone, child or adult.

"Are you hungry?" I asked him.

"Yes," he said.

So for one last time I took him to the diner and watched him drink his coffee and smoke his cigarette and eat his fries and hamburger. He wasn't angry, not even a little. He moved on, he always moved on. He didn't care that I had him arrested. He didn't care that I tried to have the judge remove him from my home. He didn't care that I pleaded with the doctors at the psychiatric ward to keep him. Thinking backwards was not his thing. What does he need tomorrow? What does he need now? That was the universe of his mind.

"I need some new jeans," he said to me.

"Really? Okay. I'll take you to the mall next week," I lied, knowing full well that his life, as he knew it, would once again come to an end. All that was left to do was to make the call and, of course, write the check. The abductors were coming again. I was short on grist and anthrax and they would provide plenty of both.

And Gabriel...he never saw it coming. He was oblivious to his fate. The court said, go ahead; kill your parents. And when you do, you will have to clean the basement along with your room. But don't worry, we'll never check up on you. That was not just what Gabriel thought, it was what he empirically knew. His MySpace page said it all. In big bold letters it read: *I am the stitch, the judge is my bitch!*

Four days later, at nine o'clock in the morning there was a knock on my front door. Three young men, none of them any larger than Gabriel, introduced themselves. I walked them up to his room. I surveyed the chaos and I said, "Gabriel, wake up." I said it again, this time squeezing his shoulder. He opened his eyes and he saw the men.

"What did I do now," he asked, still groggy.

"It's time for you to go," I answered, "Get up."

He jumped to his feet, now fully aware of what was happening. When he was fourteen and smaller and less violent, we paid two men four thousand dollars to do the exact same thing.

The volcano was about to blow. Two of the men grabbed Gabriel and forced him face down into the bed. Gabriel cried out, "You promised me! You promised you would never do this again," his voice muffled by a blue pillow, his face pressed into it, as his body struggled to free itself from the weight of his abductors.

He screamed again, "You promised. I'll fucking kill myself, Dad," his voice furious and fearful and full of the knowledge of freedoms lost. "Dad, you can't do this. You fucking can't!"

But I did. And it was easy. And I said, "Good luck" as I walked out of his room and left the house. And Paula and I went to the diner. And she had an omelet and I had French Toast with bacon and a large glass of orange juice. And when I paid the check there was a bowl of peppermints beside the cash register. I looked at Paula and thought about the truth, thought about mints and sucking and the death of our sex life and our souls. The last ten days had been among the worst, but we weathered them. That was our specialty, our strength. We always weathered the storm. We were the king and queen of bad weather.

So I shoved a handful of mints into my pocket, confident that the day would come soon when their usefulness would once again be of value.

Chapter 14

Five boys are walking. Baggy cargo shorts reach below their knees like brown paper bags that each has stepped into. Around their waists are vertical stripes, or stars or cartoon characters on the boxer shorts that rise above the beltless waistbands and rest on their hips and butts, preventing full boxer underwear exposure. They are dressed in the colors of nature—late autumn, early spring. Dirty red and faded orange t-shirts contrast their khaki-colored shorts. They move gracefully past trees, shops, and cars like mine heading in the opposite direction. They are oblivious to all but themselves, and why shouldn't they be? They are, after all, boys. Not just ordinary boys, but teenage boys—primed, packing, dangerous and wonderful.

Two boys ride skateboards. One boy walks his bike. One boy has an unlit cigarette neatly placed between the top of his ear and the side of his head. The final boy is just a boy, laughing and pushing and grabbing for the cigarette that clearly does not belong to him. And I am just a man that catches their essence in flashback of a time when I didn't hate being in love with everything they stood for.

I had a boy once, and now he is nearly a man. When he was born I named him for an angel at a time in my life when I thought that angels mattered. I brought him home and I loved him with an arrogant gluttony, a noble intensity, feeding my aspirations for his glorious future.

Now I am callous; I know I am. But today, when I see these boys and I capture their sweetness in my head, and I lock my radar on their every movement for all of twenty seconds as slowly I drive by, I almost, very nearly, forgive myself and forgive my son.

When I wasn't so angry, I wrote beautiful things. I said that I was blessed to be in the light of his smile. This is what I wrote; this is how I fell in love.

Gabriel kisses me. He laughs. He sits on my lap; arms outstretched, and kisses me once again. This time I laugh. He goes for my lips, my cheek, my nose. I turn my head, I tuck my chin in my chest, I look away so that the best he can do is reach an ear. We laugh together. His two-year-old sense of humor is as sweet as a field of apples. We play the game of dreams come true. My dreams, the dreams of being a parent.

At the hospital, the couch was hard. The vinyl made me sweat. Its four-foot length was far too short for my six-foot frame. My head rested on one oak arm and my legs draped lifelessly over the other. I was exhausted. I was sleeping when a man, an orderly I suppose, entered the room and told me to come and see my son.

Paula was crying when I entered the crowded labor room. In her arms she held Gabriel. He was slightly blue and very thin and wonderfully beautiful. Beside Paula, lying in the bed with her legs still apart was the woman who would place him with us, the one who just gave birth, and Gabriel's biological mother.

Today he calls me Daddy and I think, yes, I am. I say, "Gabriel, what is your name?" It seems like an easy question. It reminds me of the old joke about the color of George Washington's white horse. Gabriel pauses, "Come on," I say. "What is your name, Gabriel?"

"Boy!" he says.

"That's not your name! What is your name, Gabriel?"

"Boy," he says with a hearty laugh.

He's toying with me, we both know he knows. The right answer gets a kiss and a hug, the wrong answer gets a few laughs, keeps the game going. Gabriel likes his games.

When he was less than forty-eight hours old we brought him home. Legally, it was too soon to adopt him because New Jersey has a seventy-two-hour waiting period for agency adoptions. In our case, it took exactly one week. Six days of wonderment and one day of anxiety.

On the sixth day, Gabriel's birthmother called to tell us that the birthfather didn't want to sign the adoption papers. She was frantic. She didn't know what to do. She told us not to come the next day to sign, fearing that the birthfather would walk away with the baby. If she was frantic, then we were frantic too. It was a Sunday afternoon and there was no one to call. We never met the birthfather, but in twenty-four hours we would. We would drive to a church in Camden, let him see his son, and pray that he would give him back, would allow us to give the baby a better life than he could provide.

There is emptiness like no other when you want a child but cannot conceive. There is a hole in the world of the infertile couple that no pet or hobby or diversion can fill. And so, when the obvious became all too clear, we sought to adopt.

It seemed like 110 degrees in the church. We were greeted by two social workers, both of whom we had met before. One was ours, the other was theirs, representing the rights of both birthparents. We handed Gabriel to our social worker and she disappeared behind a door. He was seven days old and had lived with us for five days. We were painfully in love with him.

The windows of the church were closed. We stood alone in the sanctuary, a pair of Jews praying for happiness in a Lutheran church. A half hour later the social worker returned with Gabriel. "It's all right," she said. "Everything is fine." Gabriel was given back to our arms and our hearts.

That night we met our son's biological father for the first and only time. He touched Paula's hand and with tears in his eyes wished us good luck. On the way out, we left a ten in the collection plate. It couldn't hurt.

Adoption is not easy. For most, it is accepting the fact that you and your spouse will never conceive a child. For women this may be one of life's greatest disappointments, since women must learn to live with the loss of the physical act of giving birth. Men and women deal with it differently. Certainly, this was true of Paula and me. For her, it was a daily part of her life, and for me, it was a disappointment, but not a consuming one.

Gabriel's second birthday was attended by nine children. Children of all sizes and hues, some of whom looked nothing like their parents. They busied themselves with bubbles and cake and minor skirmishes. Like Gabriel, many of the children were adopted. Kids like any kids from families like any other. These are families created through adoption: a process, not a condition.

Gabriel is my dream, my oneness with unconditional love and testimony to happiness. He is as much my son as any child I might have conceived *with Paula. Through Gabriel our lives are unburdened from the weight of infertility. He gives us breath and nurtures our need to share our love.*

Life is funny. For most of the last eighteen years I have been inspired by Gabriel to write. When he was a wonderful child I wrote wonderful things. When he was horrible I wrote horrible things, but perhaps wonderfully. When I sent him away the first time, I was sad every day and moved by my own guilt to tell his story. Now that he is away again, I am not nearly as sad, knowing that I have protected my family. I am moved now by my clever wife and the strange normalcy of my home. None of my anger, regardless of past, present, or future, will ever diminish the intensity of the bond I feel for this human being who came to be my son. He is my son. He is my Gabriel. It's just that it's really hard to be in love when anger and resentment permeate every thought I have about him.

Why isn't he beautiful anymore? Why hasn't one thing I wished for him come true? Why hasn't love been enough? I prayed for a gentle breeze to carry him forward, never realizing the typhoon he would himself become. And when I saw it, I was frightened and I did not know why. Nature kills nurture; it slaughters it.

It's painful to not have an answer for him or me, or to watch him brew over time, building a fortress around his perfect body. But this is what Gabriel has done; he has told us that beauty is not enough. His words and deeds and acts no longer glow. They fade into a mirror of otherness as he screams at the world to accept his anger.

So I abandoned him with an aching heart as the lights went out and the crickets were chirping and my broken son had yet to comprehend that he is beautiful and life is cruel and love is not a thing to excoriate.

.

Chapter 15

I love the photographs of my family. My favorite is a group photo taken at Gabriel's bar-mitzvah. Everyone is in it: two sets of grandparents, all the cousins, all the aunts and uncles. Twenty-four people in total and lots of white teeth. It looks like we're having the time of our lives.

Among the thousands of pictures we possess are a couple of dozen family-of-five photos. I cherish each one of them. We have albums of photos from all the places we've been, developmental milestones, holidays, parties, whatever. I like to take pictures of my handsome family. It gives me pleasure when I can catch one of the boys in an uncharacteristic moment. I pose them, too, when they let me: Jonathan, standing in my wild-flower garden—Gabriel, posturing like a body-builder—Ethan dressed like John Lennon for Halloween, looking very hip.

I have a picture of me and Ethan and Gabriel and Jonathan in front of the giant globe at Universal Studios, Florida. It's just the Reiss boys, hanging out, having a good time.

I have a picture of the five of us sitting inside a tent in our backyard. It's the annual family camp out, close to home in case of emergencies. Gabriel, of course, is in charge. He is the leader of men, even if those other men happen to be six and eight years old.

"Ethan," says Gabriel, "Don't forget your pillow. Mom, do you have the cookies? Dad, you're sure all the flashlights work?" And then, not surprisingly, Gabriel directs Jonathan and Ethan to assist him in gathering every stuffed animal and puppet in the house. They are protection from the crickets and rabbits and barking dogs that make their way through the neighborhood at night. It's quite a show. It's really wonderful.

●

I haven't got a clue where perspective begins, but this much I know for sure; I haven't got any. When Gabriel was eight years old, we were fighting about something. I don't remember what. There was a lot of screaming but no cursing, his vocabulary had yet to reach the inflammatory stage. Yet how does an eight year old scream relentlessly at a parent? Why wasn't he afraid? What could we have possibly been fighting about to incense him and me, and for me to not be able to get control of him, not an ounce of control.... what—what—what? I really don't remember.

I remember that his room was blue. I remember he was standing on his bed. I remember being grateful that Ethan, who was five, didn't have to see this. He adored Gabriel and Gabriel was so sweet to him. Ethan had trouble finding words, his language development lagged behind his peers. Gabriel often helped him. And so I slammed the door to his room and found a seat on the stairs. And with my head squarely placed between my palms I pressed my cheeks upward squeezing little eggs of flesh and fat between my fingers and palms.

"He is going to kill us some day," I said to Paula. "He is going to get two bullets, that's all he'll need: one for Mom and one for Dad." So to amuse myself, I created the international human icon of a gun, my thumb upright and my index finger pointing straight out. I pushed my index finger hard against my temple, and looked Paula directly in her dark brown eyes and said, "Bang!" as my body crumbled on the industrial green carpeting that lined our hallway, bloodless, though nonetheless dead and quivering.

"You're crazy," she said.

"I am not."

Newsflash! Gabriel Reiss, of Old Fort, North Carolina (SUWS Wilderness Program), Dahlonega, Georgia (Hidden Lake Academy), Provo, Utah (Provo Canyon School), and East Brunswick, NJ (home sweet home) turned eighteen today. In an interview with myself I wrote: He was supposed to be home by 1 a.m. last night. At 11:30

119

p.m. I found him sitting in the family room watching television. At 2:00 a.m. when I checked his bed, he was gone. I sent him a text message that said, *U must think I am a moron?* To which he replied, *Nahh, I went for a walk. I really don't want to talk right now.* To which I replied, *Ur lying. I heard someone knocking. Enjoy ur night out. House is locked.* To which he replied, *No one was knocking.* To which I replied, *Good night.* Two and half hours later (4:46 a.m.), I get one final text. It reads, *WTF* (what the fuck). *It's so hot outside I went for a walk and came back and been sittin outside for 2 hours. I'm already pissed off.*

Three hours later, I wake up. I put on my clothes and go into the kitchen where Ethan is sitting at the kitchen table with his laptop.

"Ethan, have you seen Gabe," I asked him.

"Nope," he said.

But I saw him. On the morning of his eighteenth birthday, on his and my legal emancipation from each other, I saw him curled up like a squirrel in its nest, sleeping on my patio on a small grey wrought-iron chair. I approached him, just as I have done so many times before in our lives—my sleeping baby boy—and I kissed him on the head and said, "Happy Birthday, Gabriel," leaving him to the dew and the soft morning breeze and the real squirrels that scampered about him searching for food.

In the beginning there were no holes. All the holes were filled. My faith in an Almighty delivered to me a baby boy and I never once questioned the sexual identity of the possible final arbiter of my fate or was flip about the Deity's lack of communication with me. There was a baby in the house, a magnificent and charismatic child that reinforced my belief in miracles.

He glowed; it was as simple as that. And his glow was enough to be illuminating not only for a mother and a father and their pain, but for anyone who came close enough to witness his extraordinary magnetism. The smile, the hair, the face, the laugh...it was all exceptional. And it stayed that way for many years. And he walked on time. And he talked on time. And all of the developmental milestones, the things that mothers, fathers and doctors painstakingly measure to ensure nervous parents of the normalcy of their children, like sitting up or holding a bottle, were perfectly, absolutely on time. And when we lost a thumbtack in the dirty blue shag carpeting that accompanied the new room in the new house for the new big brother, he said, "Get a balloon and blow it up. Roll it on the carpeting, and when it pops, we will find the tack." Oh my God! He is a genius too. What a clever idea! What a wonderful problem solver he was!

And I have said this before, I know I have, but he is painfully adored by every ounce of living connection to the human condition. He liked puppets and hugs and being silly. And he liked to say no. He said it a lot, but every child said it a lot. And he still cried when he went to sleep. And he still screamed as if I had cut off his toes whenever it was time to leave a friend's. And he was not yet five but he had found his voice and it was dreadfully loud.

●

A grasshopper was on the tip of my shoe. I don't know how it got there because my shoe was making a 360 degree revolution every second or so as I travelled between seventeen and eighteen miles an hour on my bike. I thought I was peddling fast, but apparently not fast enough to avoid the leap of this miniature green exoskeleton. Jiminy Cricket had joined me on my ride. Pinocchio was surely not far behind. And, yes, the beautiful Blue Angel, engulfed in an aura of silver and turquoise, was just around the corner ready to turn somebody into a real boy. And Jiminy, sweet and adorable and easily crushed beneath my foot, was clinging to my leather shoe, oblivious to the wind I created as harder I pumped and faster I went. He was singing, too, as if he were a nickelodeon on a slow-moving carousel turned on its side:

When you wish upon a star
Makes no difference who you are ...

How was it that this little cricket didn't fall off my shoe? What manner of thing gave him the power to cling on and on as further I rode through the soft rolling corn covered fields of central New Jersey. And then he was gone. And the blue angel too. And how could I help but wonder if I had lost my chance for a real boy.

But I am ahead of myself. Gabriel was as real as the light of the sun with the very great capacity to nourish the infirm of heart. That was what he did for me. That was the power that I gave him until such time as he lost the capacity to discern right from wrong, good from bad, and love from hate…until he said to himself, *I will do nothing for anybody but me*, which sadly was just around the corner, but not the corner where the Blue Angel was waiting. He was ten years old but he is inching backwards to an unfathomable position as time progressed. What began with frustration and led to a fist had begat a cigarette and captured an attitude and changed a boy into something unearthly. Yet somehow, in an aberration of time, he had found it within himself to perform one final act of kindness that at the age of thirteen was anathema to each and every urge of his mind and body.

First, he accepted that he will be the center of attention. Second, he agreed to wear a suit and tie. Third, he pretended to accept the faith of his family and his conversion. Fourth, he became a Bar-Mitzvah, a son of goodness, and a man of the people of Israel. And even though it was all pretend and stood in sharp contrast to the heavy silver cross he now wears around his eighteen-year-old neck, it remained, nonetheless, the last selfless act of his cascading young life.

Oh, the unbridled pride. He did it and he did it well. He did it and mother and father and aunts and uncles and two sets of grandparents and an assortment of grungy looking grunge kids couldn't believe it was so, but it was. It was wonderful, amazing and possibly shocking. And maybe there was an ounce of pride for him, too, although it was so very hard to see as he quickly renounced the Jewish faith— quickly put on his adolescent chains and leather while disengaging from family and school and the little bits of responsibility that seem to weigh down his thirteen-year-old day.

I loved him very differently then. And yes, I sent him away. And then he came home, and then he lived, and then he destroyed, and then we sent him away again. Hope and forgiveness: beyond aspirations, barely within reach.

●

It's dark. I lie in bed with my eyes open. The windows are closed, but I can still hear the gentle midnight roar of the New Jersey Turnpike, a mere quarter-mile from the front door of my safe suburban home.

Safe, that's a joke. Walk through my house; see what my 14-year-old son had done: a pile of broken picture frames, a hole in the wall, a closet without a door, a few shards of glass still beneath a recently repaired window.

At 2 a.m. I go to Gabriel's room to check on him, and he asks me to rub his back. His skin is cool to the touch as my hand slides across the suppleness of his young developing muscles. His thick hair is the color of henna. His eyes are dark and sophisticated. He is lean and muscular and striking.

What he doesn't know is that these will be the last hours in his bed, in our house, for a long, long time. Yet he must sense something's up; he can't sleep.

I can't either. I haven't even tried.

It's been a relatively good week: no major fights, not much cursing. Our "R-rated-house," as his younger brother describes it, recently has been closer to PG, which makes this even harder. But the irresolvable problem, the breaking point for us, is that he has stopped going to school; he simply refuses. Instead he stays up late and then sleeps in and hangs around until his friends come home from school, when he leaves to join them.

Back in our bedroom, Paula says to me, "What's going to happen?"

"I don't know. I just hope he doesn't wake up his brothers."

At 4 a.m. they arrive, right on time. I open the door and hear, much louder now, the sound of cars rushing by on the turnpike. But their car, its engine cooling in my driveway, is quiet.

Two young men step out. One is big but not huge. The other is average size.

"So how do you do this?" I ask. "What if he resists?"

"It's rare that anyone resists," says the average-size one. He goes on to explain a process called de-escalation. They are experienced, bright, and articulate; they make a living going into strangers' homes and taking away their unsuspecting children to youth boot camps, private boarding schools, or, in our case, a therapeutic wilderness program. They are paid a lot of money by parents like us who hope that somehow, some way, our beautiful babies can be fixed.

We enter Gabriel's room. I press against his shoulder to wake him.

He looks up and sees the escorts. "What did I do now?"

I tell him to get up and get dressed. "You shouldn't be surprised," I explain. "You knew this is what would happen if you didn't go back to school."

He screams, "Fuck!" and punches the wall.

"We love you," Paula and I say, and then, per the escorts' instructions, we leave the room.

From our bedroom we hear the muffled sounds of conversation but can't make out the words. There is no shouting. I think I hear him crying, but maybe that's wishful thinking. I hope he cares enough to cry.

I hug Paula. We are not crying. We are too nervous to cry. How much time has gone by? Five minutes? Ten? And then footsteps, the door closing, and we look out our bedroom window to see the car making its way back to the New Jersey Turnpike.

In the morning I go to work and wait for the call to let me know he has arrived safely. I can't stay home and think about it. I need to be distracted. I need to call my parents, to explain it all to them, and in doing so accept my failure as a parent. It's not easy. My mother cries.

And then I get the call; he's there.

In the wilderness of North Carolina he will not see or speak to his friends. He will not sneak out in the middle of the night. He will not be brought home by the police. He will not come within 10 miles of a cigarette. He will not curse at us or break anything

124

of ours. He will not see a movie, have sex or go on the Internet. He will not receive phone calls from strangers. He will not get in trouble for missing school; his school is the wilderness now.

In the wilderness I will not come into his room when he is sleeping and kiss him on the head. Instead, a counselor will check on him. At bedtime the counselor will take away my son's shoes to make it more difficult for him to run away.

Every night that he's gone, I softly call out his name. I want him to know that I'm thinking of him and I'm hoping that he's thinking of me. He is, of course, thinking of me. He's thinking of his mother too. He writes us horrific letters, rife with the contempt and venom that often filled our home. They are idle threats from a frightened child. His counselors assure us that he is doing well and that in time his attitude will change. Living in a sleeping bag and under a tarp, they say, does that to a person.

Gabriel's wilderness experience will last seven weeks before we are reunited. When we do see him that first time, he is cold and nasty to us, having recently learned that he is not coming home but instead going straight from camp to boarding school. Yet that evening, before we leave for the boarding school, we spend an emotional night together in a 10-by-12 cabin with no heat, no water, and no electricity. We speak about life and family and honesty in a way we never have, and it feels like a breakthrough.

After this visit it will be another seven months before he finally sets foot in the house he grew up in. Seven months is a long time to adjust and it will not be easy for Gabriel or those of us he left behind. He has a lot of changing to do and we have to learn what normal is. His brothers miss him. We miss him. But why? He ceased to be a part of our family long before we sent him away.

Jonathan is the saddest. When we told him that we sent Gabriel to the wilderness, he began to cry and said, "But he liked me."

For several months there is a strange tension in our house; we're not sure what to do with ourselves. We're not exactly zombies, but we're shell-shocked; we need time to recuperate. We go on as if nothing has changed but the absence of what Gabriel was and what he turned us into is palatable. The boys go to school as if nothing is different. Thank God they are young. They're damaged goods but they can be repaired. I know it and watch their slow recovery. Paula and I go to work. We're damaged too. We're torn and somewhat beaten down. Yet there is a calm in our household, an eerie calm. Things no longer disappear. The crying—the screaming—the fear—the late night visits from the police—are over. The fifty dollar bill that Paula's mother sent Jonathan for his birthday, stays on his desk for weeks, exposed to the world for anyone to take. Ethan and Jonathan don't hide their money, they don't hide anything. They are not light but they are lighter. We take a vacation to Colorado and it's fun, and we do things together and without even knowing it, we are normal.

Which is not to say we don't miss him…we do. And we hope that Gabriel gets better. And we want him home when he is ready. But he is going to school—imagine that! His new world is different now. It's limited. It's structured. It's amazing what a person can accomplish when there are no distractions.

●

A full nine months after he was taken away on that awful night he is home again, and for two whole days, before he returns to boarding school, he is loved by us and by his brothers. Yet I worry that the boy we had whisked away all that time ago is still lurking under the façade of his smile.

Later, I hear him above me in his room. It's midnight, and he can't sleep. I hear his footsteps, then the sound of his door opening and closing. It's hard not to think what this meant before.

A few days earlier I visited him at his therapeutic boarding school, where he introduced me to his teachers and friends. He was confident and poised. We hugged and laughed. "How's school?" I asked. He said it was horrible, but he smiled, and we both knew that's what all the kids say.

He's not the same boy, but we don't tell him that. He has changed, but he doesn't completely see it and it's wonderful that he can't. In another year he'll see it even less.

Part of me is confident that we have done the right thing. As painful and difficult and expensive as this process has been, it's clearly been worthwhile; maybe it even has saved his life. But now, during the few days he's home, I sense the re-emergence of frightening patterns: the mess in his room, the piles of dishes in the basement where he hangs out, the pounding music. Are these signs of trouble or normal teenage behavior?

"Can you bring in the garbage cans?" I ask tentatively, probing him.

He shoots me an unpleasant look and mutters an under-the-breath remark. Still, he brings in the cans and places them against the wall in front of a gaping hole he made one day with the angry swing of a golf club.

I am quietly terrified again, but what scares me, I realize, is not his behavior but my inability to know how to read it. I have no idea what typical teenage angst and opposition look like when it comes to him, and I worry I'll never know.

Paula doesn't understand why I'm so upset. "He's been nothing short of great," she says.

And she is right. I have to believe that.

Now it's late and he's asleep; his room is quiet, dark. I walk down the stairs toward the kitchen. On the wall of the stairway is his baby portrait. I lean toward it, kiss his beautiful 1-year-old face, and pray that the worst is over.

Chapter 16

I have said horrible things about Gabriel, but he has said worse things about me. It's not a tit-for-tat or one-ups-man-ship or me trying to stick it to him after he has stuck it to me. It's where I am in my grief, if that's what I'm in, and I readily admit it. Sometimes I think I have lost my humanity and sometimes I think that everything I have done to him and for him is merely delaying the inevitable. And the inevitable, in all its permutations, is a frightening alternative. And sometimes, more often then not, I just don't care.

An alcoholic has to hit rock-bottom before he can fully recover. I'm not sure that Gabriel has hit rock-bottom yet. I'm not sure what he has to recover from. Can a person recover from being a jerk, an ass, a thief? I know he will never forgive me for hiring three men to take him out of my home when he was seventeen. And he might not forgive me for hiring two men to take him out of my home when he was fourteen. And he probably won't forgive me for forcing him to play Little League baseball either. I guess if there is something that I want him to recover from, it's his anger. Yet I don't know if that's possible for either of us. For so long I took it. I loved him; I forgave him; I protected him. I do none of these things now. Maybe love...maybe. On a good day, when the sun is shining, when I don't walk by the patched holes in my walls, when I am comforted by the sight of his one-year-old portrait, I still love him; I love him a lot.

There was a brief time when I thought I could put an end to the worst part of his life. I wrongly accepted him for who he was. I believed that love was better than jail. I had faith, endless mountains of it. He, She or It, and all of them that never spoke to me had nothing to worry about. This is what I wrote when he was sixteen, just a few months after I brought him home from his first therapeutic boarding school in Georgia: Hidden Lake Academy.

●

How many police does it take to calm down my son? One? Two? Three? The answer is nine: four police cars, each with two officers and one detective traveling solo; that's what it takes on a Friday afternoon on a busy street on a slow crime day in the suburbs. That's what happens when people with cell phones witness a sixteen-year-old boy striking a fifty-year-old man, when other people are forced to define faith in their own limited way, when strangers are compelled to respond to a drama they don't understand. They don't know that this father and son can work out their differences. They only see violence and want it to end. For them, faith is a massive show of force. It keeps them clean and safe from the struggle.

So I registered an insult to my body along with my understanding of normal human behavior and I reminded myself that this boy, this child of mine, is not normal. And I take it. As humiliating as it is, I take it—a blow to my back and smack to my forehead and a litany of insults worthy of a major ass-kicking by any normal father with any normal son acting so outrageously. And someday, I tell myself, I will do it. Someday, I will literally kick his ass. And the remorse I feel will not diminish the gratification of fulfilling my desire to cause him pain. I want to cause him pain.

He looks great, but he is in lousy shape. Cigarettes, drinking and too much ice cream after midnight does that to a person, even if that person is only sixteen years old. So I have these fantasies, a Technicolor array of revenge sequences. One roundhouse blow to the midsection and it's over in an instant—one massive uppercut—one well positioned fist to the jaw. He thinks he can take it, but I know better. I see him doubled-over on the floor, unable to return my punches. He's not nearly as tough as he thinks, and he's never been hit like this, never by a person of my size and strength. It would be so easy for me to hurt him and it would feel so good—but I don't—I can't—I won't. Not now. Not ever, reminding myself that this is an emotionally troubled boy.

I understand that there are no more reasonable questions to ask. Reason is a characteristic of normalcy and normalcy has an irreconcilable relationship with my life. How does a boy strike his father? How does a boy say *fuck you* to his parents? How does a child with so much uncontrollable rage cling to his blanket and hug his grandmother and rub my back and still call me Daddy? How does he not see that he loves me? How does he not appreciate or understand my love for him?

At six in the evening, I pick him up from work. He's been working at the car-wash for two months now and seems to like it. Certainly, he likes the money. He gets paid on Fridays and by Sunday it's all gone.

It's a Friday night when I pick him up. He gets in the car, hands me his paycheck and asks me to cash it for him. The check is one hundred and twenty-two dollars. I take the check and give him one hundred and two.

"What the fuck!" he says.

"You owe Jonathan twenty dollars. I'll give it to him for you."

"No you won't," he tells me.

"Yes. I will," I respond. "You agreed to this, remember?"

"Fuck that. Gimme the rest of the money," he screams.

"Gabriel," I say, "You have a hundred dollars. What's the problem?"

"It's my fucking money. Just give it to me."

"If I don't pay Jonathan, he will never get his money back. It's not right that you take advantage of him."

"I'll fucking pay him," he yells.

And I say, "I'll do it for you," as the transformation begins. It is instant. The cursing, the name-calling, the punching of the dashboard and window, and the kicking of any and all objects within the range of his feet, create a sum far worse than its whole. The monster is back.

So I pull into the nearest parking lot, get out of the car and begin to walk away. He is on me, stalking me with a frightening battery of threats and insults.

After fifteen minutes he sees me with my cell phone and yells at me, "Did you call the cops?"

"No, I didn't," I say.

I don't have to. The drive-by witnesses take care of that for me. Their faith is different than mine. I believe in hope; they believe in justice.

Five minutes later, two officers arrive. Within ten minutes, nine of them surround us. The first to approach is a stocky young man with a shaved head and dark narrow sunglasses. He looks like a polar bear with a buzz cut. A sixteen-year-old boy fighting with his father is hardly his dream case on a Friday afternoon. He has the look and the attitude required of a modern-day suburban police officer, but he doesn't have the crime he yearns for on a hot June day. Perhaps a burglary at one of the town's more exclusive jewelry stores or a hold-up at the Seven-Eleven? He didn't join the force to solve family disputes. He joined the force to catch real criminals doing really bad stuff. This is neither. This is just my nightmare.

"Tell me what's going on," says the officer.

"My Dad is being an asshole," says Gabriel.

"Whoa!" says the officer, who quickly assesses the situation and adds, "Shut-up and sit over there," pointing to the curb. "And if I hear another word out of you, you won't have to worry about your father any more."

Gabriel rolls his eyes in indifference, still consumed in his entitlement, but smart enough (and experienced enough) to sit down as told.

The officer shakes his head. Even he was surprised by Gabriel's arrogance. I see it in his face and think, *welcome to my world.*

I give him my name. I give him Gabriel's name. I give him our address. I tell him what happened.

"He wants money," I say, "but he owes his brother twenty bucks so I'm not giving it to him. He started losing it in the parking lot at Dunkin Donuts. He punched my car. It's new and I didn't want it damaged, so I just walked away. Then he started threatening me."

"Did he hit you?" asks the officer.

"I don't know," I say. "Maybe."

"Did he hit you?" he asks again.

"What's the difference?" I say.

"Look," says the officer. "We're not going to do anything you don't want us to do. We got a call. We have a witness that drove by and said he hit you. I just need to know for my report. Did he hit you?"

"Yes," I say. "He hit me," embarrassed to admit that I raised a son who has no compunction about striking his father.

"Can you just take him home?" I ask. "Usually, when you guys show up, it's enough to calm him down."

And then the litany of questions: How old is he? Has this ever happened before? Is he on any medication? Is there someone he can stay with? Any siblings? Where is his mother?

I say, "Sixteen. Yes. Yes. No. Two brothers. She is on her way."

I tell the policeman that Gabriel has a probation officer.

"For what?" he asks.

"Assault," I answer.

I tell him that probation is a joke. He has a curfew that he never makes. He has a therapist that he never sees. He has a house that he barely lives in. I told him that unless it is a violent crime or unless the police find me dead on my doorstep, that nothing ever happens; little changes.

Another officer is talking to Gabriel. I hear him say to Gabe, "What's your problem?" but I can't hear Gabriel's response. He wasn't sitting on the curb anymore. Another officer (they all need something to do) escorts him into a police car. I could see his face through the window. He is nervous. Good.

Paula arrives. She pulls up in her white SUV and begins to speak to one of the officers. She is so angry, so tired of all of this, so tired of Gabriel. She remembers last summer and the hell we went through leading up to his incarceration. We talked about it a lot as the school year was coming to a close, about how we couldn't go through another summer like last year. "We're out of money," I told Paula. "We'd have to borrow $50,000 to send Gabriel away again.

And then he'd be home. And then what?" I did a quick calculation in my head. It's a dark joke I like to play on myself—financial flagellation of the brain. We've already spent over $100,000 on him and I was determined not to spend any more. If we're lucky, he'll get arrested again. We joked about it, but we really wanted it, too. And we want a beach house. And we want a second honeymoon in Venice. But the underlining current of our love for Gabriel is to get him away, very far away. "If that happens," I told Paula, "he's on his own." And perversely I added, "It will happen. Just give him time."

There are a dozen people at the scene, including Gabriel. Still, I feel alone. All the police... all the cars passing by, staring at something they couldn't possibly understand. I was frozen like a mosquito trapped in amber looking out at a world I could see but couldn't control. The cars pass slowly, drivers and passengers craning their necks to get a glimpse of the wreckage of my family. They were expecting a car crash, or a homeless person passed out in the middle of the street, or a body under a blanket, a small stream of blood spreading like poison ivy across the black macadam.

I wasn't even thinking about Gabriel. I was thinking who among the hundreds of passers-by knows me? And if someone knows me, a friend or an acquaintance, would they stop to offer assistance?

Paula approaches me with one of the officers. She is angry and disgusted and in a place that I have already left. The ferocity of my anger is gone as soon as the police arrive, as soon as I know the worst is over. It was obvious to me what Paula so desperately wanted. She wanted him arrested and taken away, just like we had discussed. In many ways the abuse over the years has been far worse on her. As things got really bad, she was always the first one to call the police and Gabriel knew that. He used that knowledge in his daily taunts and verbal assaults. "Go ahead and call the fucking police," he would say with a smirk on his face, "The big, bad fucking police...They won't do shit." The bigger he got, the more worried she became that he might hurt her or one of the other boys. I could face him toe to toe, Paula could not. She would lock herself in her room, often crying, often frightened, as he pounded on the door for whatever he wanted that she wouldn't give him. And then I would get the phone call, and one of us would call the police before he started wrecking our house with his fists and his uncontrollable rage.

Gabriel did what we knew he would eventually do and now it's up to us (up to me) to incarcerate him. It is our dark and shared fantasy come true. In his own horrible way, he has given us the opportunity to free ourselves from the awful connection to our lives that he has become. We have been complaining for months that the police and the probation officer do nothing. When Gabriel threatens us, they come to our house but do not take him away. When he misses his curfew, night after night, they barely slap his wrist. When he stops taking his medication—when he stops going to therapy—when he stops caring about anything or anyone other than himself—they do nothing. Now they are saying it is up to us, up to me. The police will do whatever we want them to. Once again I have the power to direct Gabriel's fate.

"Mr. Reiss," the polar bear says, "what do you want to do?"

"Take him home," I say again. "Can you please just take him home?"

"I don't want him in my house," says Paula fiercely. "You have to press charges! Why won't you press charges?" she vehemently says to me.

I say nothing. I walk away. I look over at the police car with Gabriel sitting in the back seat. He is waving his hands across his face like a person trying to stop a car on the highway in desperate need of assistance. He shakes his head to the right and to the left and he mouths the words, "No. No. No." He knows what his mother wants, and maybe he knows what I am thinking. He is scared—temporarily, pathetically scared.

But I can't do it, I can't have him arrested. I can't go home and explain to his brothers that I locked him up—they wouldn't understand. I walk up to Paula, the woman with whom I have built a life, the woman I love, the woman who is Gabriel's mother, and Ethan's and Jonathan's, and a woman who deserves so much more than she got—so much more than me or this family—and I let her down... I know I let her down. And I say, "I can't do it. I can't have my son arrested. Not for this."

"Why not," she says, angry and pleading "Why can't you?"

"I just can't. I won't do it," I say.

And that's it. I see the disgust in her face as she turns and walks back to her car. I watch the policemen enter their respective vehicles. One of them has Gabriel, but they are not taking him home as I requested. They are taking him back to my car a few blocks away, back to the Dunkin' Donuts where it all began over twenty dollars that I wouldn't give him. For a mere twenty dollars all of this could have been avoided. My faith and my self-esteem would be intact. Everyone would be so much happier if we always did what Gabriel wanted. Another mistake...another failing on my part.

I do not have any more faith in Gabriel than the police or Paula. She is right; they are right. I should say, *take him; take him away swiftly and without prejudice. Let him sleep on a cot or the floor. Let him know that his fist will not penetrate a cinder block as easily as it does sheet rock. Let him know that he will not set foot in my car or my home or my life until there is no uncertainty that love and respect and kindness are his daily mantra.* If it requires incarceration to learn that lesson, so be it. The message is absolute. Violence is unacceptable. Violence is consequated. Violence is jail time. That's what I should do...but I don't.

There is another message, a message that speaks to a legacy of the heart I cannot accept. When given the choice, how can I possibly send him to jail? It's one thing to forcibly send your son away to a wilderness program or boarding school, where presumably he will be helped. It's another thing entirely to have him arrested. I have experienced both and they were the most awful days of my life. Not so long ago I told myself that I did these things for him, for the baby who lit up my life, for the man he will be some day, and for the love that is an endless passion. I can't do it again. I can't give him another memory of abandonment, as noble as my intentions might be.

With his life on the precipice, I'll give him a memory of absolution, hoping that some day he might show mercy himself. I'll accept him for who he is, as dangerous as that might be. On a hot day in June, surrounded by anger and confusion, when Gabriel's world is about to crush him, I will give him three gifts: First is the gift of love. Second is the gift of forgiveness. Third is the gift of understanding. I pray that these gifts sustain him through his troubling and unpredictable world and that someday my faith in him will be rewarded with a thank you at the very moment when I need it most.

●

Weeks pass; it's August. We made it through the summer, nothing worse has happened since the incident in the parking lot. I see Gabriel, but rarely. He has entered a new world of mostly invisibleness. He sleeps. He wakes. He leaves. We say very little to each other. It is an old paradigm, unacceptable when he was fourteen, but perfectly fine now that he has turned seventeen. Paula does her best to tolerate his absence, but the truth is that we like it, we like it a lot. He is out until midnight or later every night, and when he comes home he is not drunk or stoned or bouncing off the walls, which is not to say that he has not been drunk or stoned or bounced off of somebody else's walls earlier in the day. But he is coming home; everyday he is coming home. Even when we don't want him to, he does. If there was one thing that is dramatically different, this is it: I wake up in the morning and Gabriel is asleep on my sofa...always!

When he comes home at night he is hungry. He makes himself a TV dinner and turns on the television while talking on the phone or instant messaging on the computer. Like all teenagers he is facile at multitasking; he is most comfortable with sensory overload. Occasionally, he will take a break and go outside for a cigarette where the only medium available is the cordless phone. I can hear him laughing and bragging to any one of several girls who have been taken in by his charm. For a while he had a girlfriend. When she broke up with him he was miserable and ugly for several long days. Afterwards, he was only miserable and ugly when we said *no*. We still say *no* to lots of things, some we can control, (Can I have twenty bucks? No.) and some we can't (Can I go to the shore tonight? No.). So he goes to the shore and sometimes he tells us and sometimes he doesn't, but always when I wake up in the morning, he is there, asleep on the sofa, the TV on, the computer on, the phone nestled beside his gaping mouth, a small pool of saliva gathering beneath his chin.

In the morning the shades are drawn and the room is dark. Gabriel is lying on the sofa, nestled between the competing lights of the television screen and the computer terminal. He is wrapped in his blanket from head to toe. In his hand he clings to the blankie his grandmother made him when he was born. I can see a large embroidered G covering his fingers, covering his knuckles where not so long ago he'd tattooed the initials of his boarding school with a ball point pen and a thumb tack. There is a hint of sweetness in his face, a sublime reminder that this is my baby; that somewhere in that lean and muscular and often angry body, there remains a fraction of innocence, an ounce of love to be found in my son.

I want to cry. It seems like forever since I'd last captured his innocence, since I last looked at him with empathy and simply adored him for who he is. His innocence is gone forever. It has been replaced with a vile mouth, an uncontrollable temper, a penchant to steal, and fists and feet that put holes in my walls and ruin every door in my home.

He takes a deep breath. He lets out a slight cough. He rolls over and exposes the rest of his name crumpled beneath his cheek in faded blue thread. The boy who has no reluctance to threaten my life is sleeping with baby ducks and kittens and teddy bears watching over him, preserving his innocence, exposing himself to anyone who cares enough to look really really hard.

This is normal, I think to myself. This is nice. This is a teenage boy heading into his last year of high school. He likes music and cars and girls and MTV and My Space. This is normal, isn't it?

I did this once. I slept on my parents' sofa too. And one day while I was sleeping my father tried to wake me up and discovered a tattoo on my ankle. He was furious. It was 1974, long before tattoos were common. And besides that, Jews didn't get tattoos. The only Jews with tattoos were the ones who went into the ovens. My father's sons did not get tattoos. But now he had a son with a tattoo and he couldn't get it out of his head.

"Is that real?" he asked me.

"Yes," I replied, only to hear him scream out my mother's name. "It's real; so what?"

Thank God he had to leave for a round of golf. It would have been so much worse if he hadn't been going anywhere. Not that it mattered to me—why would it? I did what most teenagers did; I pushed the envelope and I got caught. Big deal! I always got caught, just like Gabriel. In the end, it barely affected me at all. It affected my father, and that was perfectly fine with me. I didn't know it, but to my father, I was invisible too. He didn't know me—couldn't know me—and I suppose he paid a small price for not understanding his son.

Finally, I see the light…the truth…something. An August morning—a grey sky—a watery mist—a breath of life asleep on my sofa. It is my epiphany, my actualization, my moment of self. All of the things that I wish for Gabriel to realize, all of the things that I should say to him but never have, never knew how, never had the knowledge or understanding or the simplicity of mind to realize what was so incredibly obvious: *everything that matters is invisible.* Hope is invisible. Love is invisible. Faith is invisible. Hate and fear are invisible too. Our passion is invisible, often trapped inside us, undiscovered by ourselves, our loved ones, our teachers, parents, therapists, policemen, judges, tutors, social workers and friends. It is the greatness of all our invisibilities that makes each of us wonderful in our own unique way.

Now I know that these are the things that matter. We cannot look at hope. We cannot see love. We cannot watch a heart shrink or grow or open or close. Gabriel is my love, my hope, my embodiment of everything wonderful, terrifying and invisible. He is Gabriel, and for now that is enough.

Chapter 17

I'm horny. It's 8:30 in the morning on a Thursday and I'm late for work. I have needs, strong fifty-year-old needs, and I have decided that they need to be met now. The boys are off to school. The house is quiet. The sun is shining and my bride of nearly twenty three years lies beside me. She is not a vestal virgin, but I am not Mr. America. We are simply Paula and Rick; it's just us.

Paula nudges me. "Do you hear that," she says.

I listen carefully. "Hear what?"

"Listen," she says.

In the distance, or at least around the corner, I hear a loud motor and the faint but screechy sound of a truck with bad brakes.

"Yes. I hear it," I say.

"Did you take out the recycling last night?" Paula asks.

"I'll take it in myself on Saturday," I say, snuggling up to her.

"There's too much. You have to do it now," she says.

"Now?" I weakly protest.

"Now." she says emphatically.

I wrap my arms around her. I pull her close, pressing against her, letting her know in no uncertain terms that there are better things to do than take out the recycling. Paula has had the flu for nearly a week and now she is better. I am better, too. I am always better, always ready, always selfishly eager to be a man to my woman. I kiss her again; it's not going well.

"Are you serious," I complain. And then she is gone. Gone like the girl in the magician's box. And the clock is ticking. And it takes me fifty minutes to get to work. And I still have to shower and dress and brush my teeth and prove to her that I am more desirable than disposing of a large yellow tub filled with plastic and glass bottles.

I don't move. I wait. I know she will be back for her morning meditation—Transcendental Meditation: Paula, the Maharishi, and me. She meditates twice a day and has been doing so for nearly thirty years. And she keeps a secret...a big secret. How can she keep a secret from me? She has never told me her mantra. If I knew her mantra, that might explain a lot. It might explain why she teases me with peppermints. My candy crunching tease of a wife floats on another plane. Tick. Tick. Tick. I have a ten o'clock meeting and I can't be late.

Paula's back. I continue to feign sleepy, pretending not to notice that she ever left. She is warm. I am warm plus. I move my mouth in an awkward dreamlike motion and kiss her neck. I wrap my arms around her once again and pull her closer, close enough to feel her heart palpitating. There is a bit of a struggle, but it's all pretend. She takes my hand (a good sign for so many possibilities) and presses it firmly between my legs, where, not surprisingly, I feel that which I wish to share with her.

"Enjoy yourself," she says with a smirk. "If you want to have sex, take out the recycling!" She gets up. She walks away. Tick. Tick. Tick.

"Paula," I plead. "This is so unfair. I can do this. I still have ten minutes. Where are you going?"

She says nothing. She is walking out of the bedroom. On the threshold she stops, turns, looks at me and says with all the confidence of a woman who has just won the lottery, "The garbage men come on Saturday."

Shoot me now! Is this what it has come to? Recycling for sex? Where is He, She or It with no name? Why does the Deity of such enormous and unspeakable power punish me in such a simplistic and cruel manner? I will save the planet tomorrow. I will.

Yet perhaps I should consider myself lucky. After all, morning sex is a new phenomenon, wholly impossible when Gabriel lived with us, and gloriously doable during his re-education in Utah. By the time we got him to school, if we got him to school at all, we were both exhausted. Whether it was a bad night's sleep or more likely a bad attitude, getting him to school was always a nightmare.

●

On the morning of the broken windshield, I stand outside of Gabriel's room. His brothers, early risers, are fed, dressed and glued to the Cartoon Network. Paula is still sleeping. There is no point knocking on the door to announce myself. At best, Gabriel's been sleeping four or five hours. He is in a deep sleep and could easily sleep until noon if not roused. So I rouse him. First, optimistically, I nudge him on the shoulder. "Gabe," I say not too loudly, "You have to get up for school." There is no response, so I nudge him a little harder. He starts to moan and tells me to go away. "Gabriel," I intone in a much louder voice. "You have to go to school."

"I'm not going to school," he informs me.

"Why not?" I ask.

"I hate school," he replies, forcing out the words as if he were spitting out poison.

So far our conversation has been relatively civil, but then I start to pull on the covers. He grabs them and screams at me, "Get out of my room!" And so the battle begins anew. It's almost daily. It's the reason I stay home in the morning and face the rush hour traffic, as opposed to leaving early and reducing the time I spend on the highway by a third. I step back; I survey the chaos he calls his room. The drawers on the dresser are broken. The closet has no door and several days of clothing conceal most of the hard wood floor. The clothing provides a soft resting place for his guitar, his drumsticks, the empty juice box cartons, and the ripped-out pages from skateboard magazines that he taped to the walls but are slowly peeling away. Every day another one drops to the floor.

"You have to go to school!" I say more forcefully, and pull harder on the covers.

"Get the fuck out of my room!" he screams back at me.

In a modulated voice, trying to stay calm, I say, "I will not get the fuck out of your room. Are you going to school? You have to go to school."

He does not reply, which I take as a good sign and step away. "We have to go in ten minutes," I say from the doorway.

A few minutes later I hear him moving about and assume he is getting dressed. When he finally emerges from his room, dressed in his fourteen-year-old's uniform of black pants, black t-shirt with a red skull, black leather bracelets, and a green overcoat on which he had drawn or written the words death and kill and several other allusions to violence, I ask, "Do you want something to eat?"

"No," he says.

"Okay. Let's go," I say, barely acknowledging our exchange, which has become so much the norm in our household that we fail to recognize how awful our lives have become.

"You missed the bus, so I have to drive you," I inform him.

"Whatever," he says.

He sits in the front seat next to me and immediately begins to press the buttons to the radio. I reach over and adjust the volume and he likewise does the same until an unhappy compromise is found. A few minutes later we pull into the school's parking lot.

"Okay, I'll see you tonight," I say, but he doesn't move. "Gabe, get out of the car." He is motionless. "Gabe, I have to go to work. What's the problem?"

"I'm not going to school. I just remembered I have in-school detention, so fuck that."

"That's not my problem," I say. "You have to go to school! You have to go to school!" It's my mantra and it's not working. Paula's secret mantra puts her mind at ease. My mantra is an invitation to escalate a battle. The more I say it, the more aroused he becomes. There is no point trying to be rational. Gabriel is not a person for whom rationalizing makes any sense. His mind is not trained to work that way.

"If you don't go to school, then you have to go to work with me. I will not leave you home alone for the day."

"Fuck that!" he screams at me.

"Are you going to school?" I ask again.

"Fuck school!"

143

"Then you're coming with me."

"Fuck you!"

I am pulling out of the parking lot. "Take me home," he says.

"I am not taking you home, you are coming with me." And so he begins to punch the door and scream. He bangs the dashboard with his fists. He punches the window. He realizes that we were not heading home but toward the highway. "Take me home, Goddamn it!" he screams again.

"Go to school," I repeat.

"Fuck you and fuck school. I hate fucking school." He begins to kick and flail. And I know that I have seen this before and sometimes he can stop and sometimes he can't. And he's not the baby who was my salvation, he's not the beautiful cherub whom we all adored, and he's not the boy with the magnetic laugh. He is a monster. And then his foot breaks my windshield and I become him.

"What the fuck is wrong with you?" I scream. "I can't believe you broke my Goddamn windshield." I am driving with my left hand and with my right hand I reach across the seat and begin to beat him on the legs. I can see that he's calmed down, (even he can't believe that he broke my windshield) but that doesn't stop me.

Under his breath I hear him say, "I'm sorry." It's barely audible and I suppose it took a bit of courage to say, but what am I supposed to do? So I stop hitting him. I can't hit him forever. It doesn't do a bit of good and I still have to drive the car to get to work. And then when I get to work I have to call the school and tell the school that he is with me. And then I have to tell Paula. And how can I tell her that he broke my car window? I can't. It's too much. In the silence (thank God we are both silent) all I can think of is that I will get through this day just like I got through yesterday and just like I will get through tomorrow. It is the best I can do for the moment.

This is my life, my journey—thrilling and terrible and out of control, suffocating all hopes for an ordinary family.

●

Now it is ordinary. Sometimes I have sex in the morning. Sometimes I have sex at night. And sometimes I take out the recycling and the garbage, and I don't feel bad, not one tiny bit. This is not to say I don't miss Gabriel. I do. I miss him terribly. But I miss having a life, too. I miss living in peace and not having to worry about the safety of my family.

There was a time when I would lie in bed late at night and send telepathic signals of love to wherever Gabriel might be. He was in boarding school or wilderness or maybe he just decided not to come home on a particular night. Perhaps he was high, or drunk or with a girl? It didn't matter to me; it was the message that was important. When I asked him if he ever got any of my messages, he said no. It's too bad, really. I wanted him to know and feel the intensity of my love. I thought that love, even telepathic love, had the power to make a difference, but I was wrong.

In Gabriel's journals he writes about love. His love is different than mine. It's adolescent. It's for a girl. Yet it's so important to him that he writes about it often. Ironically, he cannot see or feel the love that surrounds him. He doesn't understand the importance of the things that are invisible. Who knows what he is thinking now? Perhaps he is feeling the hate. I'll just be glad if he is feeling anything at all. I pulled this from one of his journals:

Love is a strange thing,
It takes you places you've never been.
It makes a light shine in your mind.
I miss life more than I miss myself.
I miss love so much that it hurts.
My heart is bleeding.
I hope she has the cure.

Chapter 18

It's a dream—my dream—real, not made up. The first thing you have to know about the dream is that I am aware of being in a dream state. I know that there must be some significance to this awareness, although I have yet to determine what that might be. Why would I know I'm dreaming? Why would I need to know? What does this tell me about my subconscious if my subconscious is not working subconsciously? It kills me to admit it, but even in a dream state, conscious or otherwise, I feel hopeless. If I am going to dream, let me at least be oblivious.

The dream is not good; it's unpleasant and makes me nauseous. On a certain level it is frightening, but clearly not frightening enough to qualify as a full-fledged white knuckle nightmare—not yet. I wonder if it's really a dream at all since I am so aware that I am dreaming. Yet when cognition comes into play…when I reach that point where hammer and thumb painfully collide, my only reality is the agony searing up my arm, not the confusion in my cerebral cortex which has yet to discern whether or not I dreamed at all. If it isn't a dream, if these thoughts and emotions are real, then I have done something horrible. So I tell myself it's a dream…a bad dream, but not a nightmare—a dream that I can recover from. I've done that before.

In 1976 I got some really bad dope and freaked out in a room full of eighteen-year-old potheads. I was certain that I would never stop feeling the powerful thumping of my heart in my mouth and I was convinced that my sanity was lost forever. In a day or so, the normal rhythm of my heart returned. In a year or so, the flashbacks subsided and through sheer optimism I convinced myself that my brain and I would go on to lead normal lives.

In my dream I am convinced that I am awake. I feel it at my very core. But I am troubled because in my altogether not awake state I know that I have done a bad thing. I have committed murder. It is my dark and horrible secret: I, murderer. It tears me apart on two levels: first, how can I live with this horrible burden, and second, how awful is it that my subconscious has given me a conscience? I don't want to care; caring represents the antipathy of my cavalier life. I yearn for the real dreams of my youth, pre-1976 adolescent dreams when I woke up thrilled and moist and exhilarated. When I would run and run and run and run and never lose my breath, never need a moment's rest, and never worry that the guy behind me would catch me. There was no guy behind me; I was uncatchable; I was invincible. I was dreaming.

This is what I know about my current dream. I have not killed Gabriel; this is not a dream about him. I have not killed Paula or Ethan or Jonathan. And I have certainly not killed the unspeaking and asexual Almighty who taunts me through silence. This is not about them. It is all about me. It is my angst, my guilt, my horror and fear. Yet I don't know who I have killed; I only know that I have. There is a murder and a murderer, and I am intricately woven into the fabric of this death.

I want desperately to let it go, but the dream is repeating itself. And so, night after night, when I rise in the morning, (if I have actually been asleep) I am mortified by my deadly act.

"Rick," I hear a voice say, "We need $5 million to complete the construction of the new dormitory." (It's Bob Mendelson, Chairman of the Board of Trustees.) "Can you think of some people we can approach who would like their name on a new building?"

What? I hate work dreams, especially when I know I'm dreaming. What a horrible intrusion of my slumber! Not that it matters. I can't answer the question anyway. My head is whirling. I am a murderer. I have to tell someone. I can't tell anyone. Five million what? Bob who?

The dream continues. Now I'm in the mountains with Ethan. He is my hiker, my adventure boy. I take him places that Jonathan won't go. He is asking me questions. He says, "I was reading this book the other day that my teacher told me to read. She said that even though it was old, it was really famous. I can't remember its name, but it's about a kid named Holden. Have you ever read it?"

My murder-obsessed mind is stunned. Ethan hates to read. He spends most of his free time jumping from one adolescent Web-site to another. And he wants to talk to me about *The Catcher in the Rye*? Now that's a rarity! I wrote my thesis about this book! Sure, let's talk. Let's bond as we have never done before over a literary classic. But I can't. My mind is unilaterally converged on the act, the death, the guilt. How will I hide this forever? How will I speak to anyone in a dream or awake until the anguish that is my shame, my lack of contrition and confession, is dealt with by a power of lesser or greater or unfathomable silence?

I know what I *should* do. I should confess to Ethan. I should wrap my arms around this sweet and thoughtful little boy—this child with his own set of real concerns—concerns that I could not fully attend to because of you-know-who—and I should say that I'm sorry: sorry for what you have seen and for what I have become and for all of the love I forgot to lavish on a child that would let me. I should whisper in his ear that I love him and would he please forgive my murderous soul.

But I can't. The dream never ends. As much as I want to control the dream, the dream is controlling me. Ethan is gone. I can't confess. He can't forgive me. He is awake and I am not with him and my subconscious mind does not even acknowledge that all I want to do is cuddle up beside him and smell the delicious nectar that is him.

And now the dream shifts again. Jonathan and I are falling. It's a falling dream and at first I think there are two of us. But no, I am not with Jonathan as I had thought; I am Jonathan. I see everything he sees. I feel everything he feels. I am him and we are not afraid. We are two people nocturnally joined as one, as an endless wind pushes a tear out of our eye. We feel it going in the wrong direction, moving upward and across our brow into the thick red hair that is

Jonathan's calling card.

Yet we are not confused. We see many of the things that define our thirteen-year-old life. We're a bit like Dorothy in the farm house as it spins and twirls and hurls itself slowly toward Oz. Yet instead of a cow we see Jonathan's laptop. His latest digital movie, Retro Gaming 2008, is playing on the screen. "Hey kids," he screams like some miniature game show host. "Remember when you had to pay fifty cents to play Super Mario Slam at the arcade. Here at Retro 2008, we've got all your favorite arcade games, and they're FREEEEEEEEEEE! Come on kids, let's play." And the camera pans my basement in all its glorious green and blue and red and purple and black and pink splatter colored walls, and stops at the little color television that is the focal point of no less than five of Jonathan's friends, all of whom are completely engrossed in a twenty-five-year-old video game.

And then we see Jonathan's red bike, and someone is riding it. It's Gabriel and he is grinning ear to ear, wearing the New York Giants jersey that I bought him in Korea just a few weeks ago. He waves at us and yells, "I'll bring the bike back tomorrow. I promise I will." We both know better.

We see books and uprooted trees, and a girl with stringy black hair, (Does Jonathan have a girl friend? A goth girlfriend?) and my mother sitting on one of my wrought-iron patio chairs reading a book. She looks up, smiles, and returns to her reading, seemingly oblivious to that fact that there is no end to our descent. But it's cool, it's fine, it's fun to be falling without fear, without worry of imminent death. And I am Jonathan, or he is me, and I kind of like it.

And then I wake up. Dream over, but at least I knew I was dreaming. And I run my fingers through my hair and a fine strand of grey gets caught in a crack in the fingernail of my middle finger, confirming that I am me and not Jonathan. And for once I have a dream where I am not obsessed with the murder. At least, not until I wake up. And then I realize that the murder has entered my waking state too. So I force it out of my mind and return to my writing, knowing very well that my real confession cannot be far behind.

●

I am curious; I am a curious person and recently my curiosity has taken me to an ugly place. I know it's ugly but I go there nonetheless. I am curious to know how many children have murdered their parents. It's important to me. It's information I must have. I want to be safe; I need to be safe. I want to know what the likelihood of my son killing me will be, and, truthfully, I'm surprised that other parents are not as burdened as I am by this nagging question. It happens; we all know it happens—a couple of shot-gun shells lying beside the swimming pool with the words Mother and Father etched into their red serrated plastic casings. A couple of bodies in the pool, floating aimlessly as the automatic pool vacuum and its long white hose twirl the bodies round and round in the pink water. A police man rubbing his forehead trying to understand the scene. A dog whining for its dinner. A family shattered. A pool waiting to be emptied.

I can't let it go. The notion feeds my dreams and keeps me awake when I should be asleep. Mothers and fathers are dying at the hands of their children, dying across the American landscape— victims of love—victims of hate.

I need an explanation. I yearn for the invisible one, the sexless one, the unknown arbiter of my subconscious to do the right thing and tell me. Why is that so difficult when it seems so simple? All that I really want is confirmation of what I already know: the world is insane...hopelessly insane. And me? I am desperate and confused and not remotely capable of dealing with the onslaught of emotions that might very well drive me to madness. Should I get ahead of the curve? Should I take him out before he does me in? Gabriel is too old, too big and too independent to slowly poison or starve or kill in a silent or insidious way. It would have to be messy like a gun or a baseball bat. So I keep praying. I keep praying to the great unknown, hoping that soon, perhaps, very soon, he will simply move out (Gabriel, not the unknown master of my silent torment.) In the meantime, I'm playing basketball in the driveway with Gabriel. We play for nearly an hour. He's really good and beats me easily. He has a nice jump shot and a good eye and even though I am five inches taller than he, he has no trouble getting around me. So maybe there is a redemptive feature within him yet? Maybe I don't have to kill him and he doesn't have to kill me. Losing is no big deal. Losing is cool when it's time spent with your son. When he is normal like this, I hold out hope. It's a stretch and I cling to it. But something else is clinging to me, something I learned that is altogether unsettling: In the history of the United States of America there have been approximately 500 serial killers. Of those 500 killers, 16% of them were adopted. Yet only 3% of all people in America were adopted. Translation: the odds of Gabriel becoming a serial killer are five times greater than that of my other children. The likelihood is infinitesimal, of course, given the billion or so people that have populated our great nation over the last four hundred years. Yet FIVE TIMES GREATER! I am out of my mind and He who does not speak to me allows it to be so.

I am a murderer and my son is not far behind. I wonder what Maurice West would say. He would probably say that it's not Gabriel's fault. He would remind me that if I wasn't made fun of as a child, and that if I didn't berate my son much as my father did me and his father did him, and so on and so on and so on, that Gabriel, instead of wrecking my house, would likely be taking cello lessons from an elderly gray-haired woman whose ancestors were all kind and generous.

Then it dawns on me. It's not Gabriel at all; it's me. Maybe I am the serial killer. Maybe I am the adopted son. How many times did my parents tell me that they found me in a garbage can? It's one of those childhood questions you never forget. "Mom. Dad. Where was I born?"

"We found him in the garbage, by the subway. Isn't that right, Renee?" says my father not addressing me directly. And my mother, she says nothing as she flips a burger in the heavy metal skillet filled with Crisco and ground beef.

For a long time I thought it was just a bad joke, but now I wonder if they were telling the truth. "Mom? Dad? Why couldn't you just level with me?"

It seems so obvious. The more I think about it, the more I see each clue to my fate. Consider this: there was a time when I owned a buck-knife and a shot-gun and a motorcycle. There was a time when I liked to blow things up and set things on fire. There was a time when my clothes were tattered and my future was uncertain and without any foreknowledge to the pain I would someday endure in my own personal hell, I forgot who I was. But now I remember everything. I know who I am.

My breathing is heavy. My pulse is zooming like a racecar coursing through my veins. What I know to be true is that I have killed my soul and now it comes back to haunt me in my dreams. I am a murderer, the serial killer of my own goodness. I have plunged that knife deep within me and only an act or sign or blessing from the invisible one can ever restore that which I have removed from myself. I am sorry. Truly, I am. I am dead.

Chapter 19

Ethan and Jonathan would like a dog. It's second on their list of life's most important things after a swimming pool.

"We promise," they say in unison, big wide smiles on their faces, "We promise, you won't have to do anything. We'll take care of it, Dad. Really, we will."

I say, "I don't need a dog. I have you."

"Ha! Ha! Very funny Dad," says Ethan in a deep monotone voice. "You're really funny, you know that."

Jonathan sidles up to me. Here we go. Mr. Sunshine is ready to lay it on thick.

"Dearest father," he intones. "Best looking Dad...Handsome Dad...Dad with a full head of thick hair who takes us to great places like Colorado (After our summer vacation in Colorado both boys swore they would never go camping with me again.) and Utah (After our vacation in Utah both boys swore they would never go hiking with me again.) and who buys us really cool stuff like dvd's and new bikes and takes us to the movies...you had a dog once. You loved that dog. I know you did. What was his name? Casey? Right? Wouldn't it be great to have a dog just like Casey?"

I'm stoic. I push him away and walk into the kitchen. If only he knew. I see a drawer that is slightly ajar and I open it, taking out a large twelve-inch carving knife.

"Do you see this knife, " I say, holding it in front of my face, twisting my wrist slowly so that the light from the ceiling lamp reflects off the blade and hits the faces of Ethan and Jonathan. "If we ever get a dog... if a dog ever shows up at our house... I will take this knife and shove it through my heart until I am dead... and you will be fatherless, but at least you will have a dog... if that's what you really want."

They are angry. I am angry too. How can we not be? Anger has been the dominant emotion in our home since Gabriel returned from boarding school nearly two years ago. And although we have sent him away again, the 80% of us who are left behind can't let it go. We need to fill the angry void that was created when he was taken away. It doesn't matter that we're safe. Our view of the world is changed forever.

Every now and then I check in with Ethan and Jonathan. I ask them if they're okay. They say that they are, but clearly they're not. I see it in their eyes. The eyes that once were filled with wonderment are cautious and observant, never knowing when the hammer will drop or the police will arrive or the ringing phone will lead to another fight.

When I ask Jonathan to clean his room and he says, "No." When I ask him again, he tells me to "Shut-up!" I want to react but I know better. This is not Jonathan; this is one boy's inability to adjust to a vicious world. He is not vicious. He is kind and confused and it will take time for him to understand that fighting is not the norm. And the saddest thing of all—the piece that breaks my heart as much as anything else I have lived through—is that I know they will never love Gabriel again.

No wonder they want a dog! They need to redirect their misplaced love but I won't let them. They don't know it, but their anger pales compared to the rage I carry with me every day. Ethan and Jonathan want a dog. Gabriel wants his freedom. And I, (standing before my fourteen- and twelve-year-old sons as I rant about suicide with a knife in my hand) would be the happiest person on the planet if I could just forget everything.

Nothing makes sense. I show Paula what I have written recently and she says in a voice that is not too kind, "The only time you write about me is when you write about sex or my body."

"That's not true," I say. "I have said some very nice things about you."

"It's not enough, write some more," she goes on.

"Okay, I'll make up something good; how 'bout that?" I say.

"No!" she shouts. She's not happy. She gives me the look. It's not a look that makes me feel very comfortable.

"Is it bad that I write about your body?" I say. "I love your body. Not only do I love your body, but we have a good sex life. What's wrong with that?"

She doesn't answer. She's conflicted and I know it. Proud as she is in the fact that her A cups have blossomed into B cups as her 50th birthday looms on the horizon. It's good. It's great. She knows it. We know it. At least I don't say that our sex life sucks and that she is an ugly shrew. I don't exploit her; I tell only the truth.

One truth that is hardly titillating at all is that Gabriel will turn eighteen in less than five months. His dreams of emancipation (which are now my dreams of emancipation) will come true. Nobody is angry. Everyone is frightened.

Where will he live? What will he do? How will he fulfill his dreams of returning to New Jersey from Utah if I don't buy him a car or a plane ticket or a ride on a bus or train? Will he disappear? Doubtful. Will he haunt me forever? Probably.

I force him out of my mind. The more he is away, the less I think about him. So much for absence making the heart grow fonder. I've grown accustomed to not seeing his face. His absence is brutally lovely and peaceful. In time, there is a calmness of spirit, mind and living that I can control. I am finally in control and it's wonderful.

The past is a sweet memory of magical moments when released from the burden of Gabriel's reality. This morning, in fact, as I opened my eyes, and pulled my hand off of Paula's warm shoulder, I was reminded of that day so many years ago when Paula and I wed.

●

I rolled off the mattress on the floor that served as my bed. It was a sunny day and a dusty beam of light emanating from the small space between the window shade and the window sill diagonally crossed the room and warmed my face. I sat up. I looked at the clock and thought, *I really need a bed. Paula will want a bed. Married couples have beds and furniture and china and children. I own a bike, a car, a mattress, a TV and a big chair. Where am I gonna put my bike when Paula moves in? I don't even have a garage.*

In the bathroom I brushed my teeth and relieved myself. I looked in the mirror. At twenty-eight my dark hair had been receding for ten years, but I was pleased that most of it was still where it belonged. I was six feet tall. My eyes were speckled with green and yellow and brown, and my body retained most of its athletic youth. I run. I bike. I lift weights. I have never forgiven myself for quitting the wrestling team in college and to lessen my guilt I worked out incessantly. I swore to myself that no matter how things went after the wedding that I would never give up working out. I would never allow my future family to encroach on that corner of my life. Exercise was more than my drug; it was the only activity that secured my sense of freedom in the world of responsible adults that beckoned me to join them.

The forecast called for a warm June day but at 7:00 a.m. there was a nip in the New Jersey air. The ground was wet with dew and a low fog covered the open field that surrounded the house of my basement apartment. I walked out the door and began to stretch for my morning run. I locked my hands behind my legs and lowered my head to my knees. I leaned against my car and stretched my calves, my body diagonally opposed to the vehicle like the dusty beam of light that woke me a short time before. I ran in place. I jumped up and down. I felt my heart beating faster as slowly I challenged my body to ready itself for the demands of the run. I could feel the blood flowing more quickly through my veins. And then, as if a silent gun went off in my head, I sprinted down the long driveway into the street. My oversized, tattered sweatshirt swayed to the right and the left with each stride. My arms, like opposing pendulums, moved in unison. And my legs, in perpetual motion, glided over the pavement.

Two miles into it, the endorphins kicked in. I didn't feel my breathing or my heart beat or the pounding of my feet on the pavement. I didn't think about work or Paula or the wedding as my body clicked into human cruise control. There was the wind that I created as I moved through space, and the homes that I passed, and the trees in full bloom, their many shades of green coming to life with the sun's rising. There was a dog that barked and a car that honked, but mostly there was nothing on this early Sunday morning. There was the run and my empty mind. Just the way I liked it.

Forty minutes later I was back, sweatshirt tied around my waist, t-shirt clinging to my sweaty body. I smiled. I breathed a good long heavy breath and pressed my palms to the ground, feeling a slight but pleasant burn in my hamstrings. I took a shower.

It's not like I didn't love Paula. I did. I loved her very much. She was pretty. She was smart. She was funny. And I knew she wouldn't bore me like so many of the women I dated before her. Even so, as I stared in the mirror I wondered, *What if I just don't go? What if instead of driving 75 miles east to Long Island, I drive 75 miles west to the Poconos? What's the worst that could happen? A broken heart. A very angry would-be father-in-law. A hundred or so gifts never to be opened. How bad was that?*

A cool sweat gathered on my forehead as I lathered my face with shaving cream. Sweat dripped down my nose and over my eyes and on to my cheeks, creating miniature rivers through the white menthol cream. Slowly I drew the razor from my sideburns to my chin, pulling away the sweat, the cream and three days of beard that made my face feel more like sandpaper than skin. I was careful not to cut myself, and when I was done, I rinsed my face with cold water and stared once again into the day, knowing that in less than five hours I would have a wife.

On the other side of the Hudson River, on a body of land not attached to the contiguous United States, they were preparing the hall. The tables were being set. The flowers were being arranged. And the simple linens and silver and glass would complete the room. It would be a pretty affair but not too elegant, and that was just fine with me.

I had almost nothing to do with the wedding plans, although

at Paula's request I designed the wedding invitation. The first design was resoundingly rejected by her parents, but Paula insisted that I try again, hoping to show off her future husband's creativity. Thankfully, the second effort, with our names in Hebrew beneath an ancient synagogue, a dove flying above, and the words, *I am my beloved and my beloved is mine*, from King Solomon's Song of Songs, creating an ornate border in Hebrew calligraphy, was met with universal approval. That was the outside of the card; it was, if nothing else, personal and unique. On the inside, however, there was a mistake. Paula's parents were listed second even though they were paying for the wedding. Not only were they listed second but their names were set in smaller type size than my parents'. By the time the error was discovered, it was too late to fix. I tried to be philosophical—shit happens. But her parents were justifiably upset. Still, I knew what my job was, and this was not it. My job, my one and only job, was to show up. I may have been wavering for a moment, but as the ceremony drew nearer, I knew exactly what I had to do.

I thought about Paula as I dressed myself in my double-breasted, charcoal-grey suit. I was sure that she was thrilled that the sun was shining on her wedding day. The weather had been horrific, grey and wet and cold for several days, but today, for her, the clouds dispersed and the sun shone through, bringing with it the warmth of the last day of June 1985.

I pictured Paula and her parents in their Long Island home as they laughed and joked and readied themselves for the big event. I could see them sitting at the kitchen table with their coffee and bagels, anxiously waiting for the wedding to begin. They were nice people. Paula's mother taught seventh grade English and her father was a high school guidance counselor. They enjoyed each other's company, and I liked watching their lively conversations, although I rarely joined in. They were talkers; they were very big talkers and had often and unintentionally made me feel uncomfortable. They were not intimidating; they were just overwhelming for a young man from a family where open dialogue was not encouraged.

I towered over Paula and her parents. Her mother was barely five feet tall, and her father was perhaps another six inches taller than that. Yet I was inherently shy and although I forced myself to overcome my shyness in the workplace, I felt less compelled to do so for my future bride's family, hoping instead that they would accept me for who I was.

Paula was adored. She was the youngest of three children and the family's only daughter. She had a Ph.D. Her brother had a Ph.D. And her other brother had a Ph.D. and an M.D. Yet because she was the youngest and because she was the girl and because she had genuinely endeared herself to everyone, she was the focal point of the family's adoration.

I, too, was the youngest of three, but it was hard for me to think of myself as the focal point of anything. My father was a stern man and a harsh ruler of the house. My mother, whose love for the children was obvious and unconditional, appeared to do whatever my father requested of her. I lived in a tense and quiet household where I was rewarded for my athletic prowess and ignored for my creativity. Mostly, I felt out of place in the house where I grew up. This wedding, this marriage, created through the promise of love, offered not only a wife, but a family that communicated and genuinely liked to spend time with each other. My future was hopeful and frightening and waiting for me on the other side of three parallel rivers just a few miles apart. All I had to do was get there.

While I dressed alone in my dingy apartment, Paula was surrounded by the love of her family. My best man, my brother, was with my parents and his pregnant wife, expecting their first child. And the few friends, with whom I'd had drinks the night before, had each returned to their respective wives or girlfriends. There was no one there to shore up my confidence. Still, as I straightened my bow tie, aligning it along the same plane as my shoulder blades, I knew that I had made the right decision.

Under the chuppah, the wedding canopy, I waited for my bride-to-be. The sun had risen and with it the temperature. The maid-of-honor, me, the best man and my parents, waited for Paula to make her entrance. A minute passed—maybe two—and then I saw her standing between her mother and father. The proud parents were beaming and so was she. They kissed her and walked toward me but I did not see them. I walked right past my future mother and father-in-law, and even though I had seen Paula in her wedding gown before, and even though we spent no less than an hour taking photos earlier in the day, and even though we had lived together in Ohio for nearly two years before I moved back to New Jersey, it was as if I had seen her for the first time and had fallen in love all over again.

She wore a simple white gown, a wreath of flowers in her hair and a smile that was nothing short of wonderful. As I looked at her, my eyes welled-up and my heart pounded. I returned her smile and took her hand and led her to the chuppah where the rabbi, the same rabbi we had known in Ohio where we met at the Hillel House of Ohio University, said, "I have known Rick and Paula since they met. And isn't it funny that a girl from Long Island and a boy from New Jersey had to travel all the way to Ohio to meet each other and fall in love." Everyone laughed and the ceremony began.

When it was over, the rabbi placed a small glass wrapped in a napkin on the ground. I knew what to do. With one strong downward step I crushed the glass, symbolizing the destruction of the Jerusalem Temple thousands of years ago and my commitment to the Jewish faith today. There was a loud pop and 120 wedding guests shouted *L'Chiam*, To Life! I wrapped my arm around Paula, pulled her close to me and kissed her on the lips, smiling all the while.

We walked through the crowd, oblivious to the photographer, the applause and the happy faces that surrounded us. We were escorted to a small room where we could experience alone our new and mutual state of matrimony. Paula read her vows, expressed her love, her longing and her hopes. She cried again.

She said, "I never stopped wanting you, caring for you, or needing you."

I said, "All that I do, now and forever, I do for you."

A few days later, on the Fourth of July, on the day before we were to leave for a two-week honeymoon in Italy, we had an intimate picnic in a field with a few thousand others waiting for the fireworks to begin. It was a crisp and pleasant evening as we listened to the New Jersey Symphony Orchestra play a medley of patriotic songs and show tunes. The picnic basket, a gift from Paula's brother and sister-in-law, was filled with cheeses and salads, and as the sky grew darker, the music ebbed and loud thunderous explosions, hundreds of feet in the air, signaled the beginning of the fireworks. We held each other's hands and looked skyward. On a star-lit night, heady from wine, our minds were free from worry and filled with the anticipation of our journey abroad and our journey through life.

We watched as crimson red, emerald green, orange and blue and lavender and gold explosions of light fill the evening sky. Each singular rocket, alone or in pattern, was another excuse to ooo or ahh, or shriek with delight. We were happy. We were happy that our journey though life together had begun.

Chapter 20

My father is dying. We are all dying, but he is closer to death than most of us. He is eighty-three and likes to tell stories about his service in World War II. He was a dental assistant in a M.A.S.H. unit before they were called M.A.S.H units. He enjoys telling me how all the nurses preferred to have him work on their teeth because he leaned in too close and unknowingly rubbed against their breasts. According to my father, the women were much hornier than the men and found his style of oral cleansing preferable to that of his peers. Beyond breasts and what he didn't tell me, I don't think he saw any action. Yet the closer he gets to death, the braver he becomes. He tells me how he landed on the beach but there was no one there to defend the island. He tells me how he scouted for the enemy but the enemy was not to be found. He tells me that once he went on a really long hike and it was really hot and he was really scared but nothing really happened. Nonetheless, he is proud to be a war hero because in today's world all living veterans are living heroes.

I want to be sad about my father's approaching demise. I know it's my responsibility to respond normally to his death, but I am not nearly as sad as I think I should be. Is it because he punished me with a strap when I was a child? I was hardly the only kid on my block disciplined with leather. Is it because he could be domineering? Is it because he is wealthy? Who knows? I try to do what's right for my mother. But just as I often wished for Gabriel to go away, I often wished the same for my father...but certainly not death; even I am not that heartless. Yet he was such a difficult man to live with...harsh and often unrelenting. It was not uncommon of me to think that the angry man who had raised me had somehow become reincarnated in Gabriel. He is a piece of my punishment pie. He is the last slice of my apple tartness.

My mother isn't saying much. Does she see the light at the end of the tunnel? She adores my father and revels in his many comebacks from near-death. I'm thinking that perhaps she got a message from Him, Her or It? The Silent One said to her that she has been a good woman and has many years ahead to enjoy. She has earned the peace that is coming and joyfully she can be patient. She is lucky. She has a voice, a faith, an understanding. I have nothing.

I am on my way to the hospital and I'm writing my father's eulogy in my head. As the so-called writer in the family I know that I will be blessed with this wonderful task. It will not be easy to say nice things about him. I decide that it will be best to tell the truth—that works. I'll say my father was a passionate man. I'll say he preferred The Three Stooges to The Three Tenors. I'll say he loved his grandchildren, but when he was coming out of my grandmother's birth canal he mysteriously lost the gene that enables human beings to listen. He is not a listener; he is a talker. And when he talks he is often not nice.

He says things like, "You don't know what you're talking about," with an awful look of disgust on his face. "Listen to me," he shouts, fully unaware that he was born himself without that aptitude.

Like so many of the role models in my life, I strove to be his antithesis. He said black, I said white. We do not complement each other; we oppose each other. He is not my ying and I have never been his yang. Thankfully, to the extent that any of us can ever escape the power of our parents, (the wonderful need to break away and the horrible need to want to please them) I have done so...sort of. I have also taken his money when I needed it. It's callous, I know; add it to the long list of my human imperfections. And when he is gone, and when my mother joins him, I will accept his largesse one final time for as long as I shall live. Ethics, you say? Integrity, you query? Apparently, I lack both, and for a very good reason. Let me think. Let me think. Oh, right—it's all about the money.

But this is not about me. Well, maybe it is.

No. No. This is about the man in the hospital bed next to my father. He is cold and asleep and shriveled. And one eye is open and one eye is closed. And he moans as if he has just witnessed the execution of his family. He wears a cap that is cotton and brown against pale blue sheets as he lies in his plastic hospital bed in a semi-fetal curl. The cap keeps him alive, keeps life from slipping out through his skull.

"Ooooooooooo! Errrrrrrrrrrr! Ahhhhhhhhhh!" Even with my eyes closed and the beep beep beep of my father's heart monitor, I readily comprehend that these are not moans of sexual pleasure; these are the moans of death.

My father, not yet dead, is disgusted; he can't stand the noise. He has agreed to pay an extra $150 a day for a private room, but he has yet to be moved.

"Grrrrrrrrrrrrrr!" moans his roommate yet again.

My father says to me, "How's the other one doing." The other one is Gabriel. Names are harder for him now. The other one is the one who is not around; it must be Gabriel.

I'm not listening. The familial missing gene has passed from father to son. I am staring at the moaner, the sleeper—his body is barely perceptible under the sheets. My father speaks again. He says, "Ricky. How is Gabe?" perhaps knowing I was not listening the first time. Yet all I can do is stare at the man in my father's matching plastic bed. I see that this man beside him, this man in his loneliness, is Gabriel's future.

If...and it's a big if...Gabriel can survive that long.

1. I am leaving the hospital with Gabriel; he is two days old.
2. I am playing with a baby whose energy and laughter carries me.
3. I am carrying Gabriel on my shoulders everywhere.
4. I see Gabriel at pre-school graduation. He prefers to sit away from the other children.
5. I visit Gabriel's classroom. He cannot sit still, not for a second.

6. Gabriel is sitting on the curb with a stuffed animal and a tiny blue suitcase on his way to his first sleepover. I take his picture.
7. Gabriel has conquered two-wheel transportation and discovers a new world.
8. I take him on vacation to Florida. He is a nightmare.
9. I take him on vacation to Utah. He is a nightmare.
10. I take him to a shrink. He is an expense.
11. I answer the phone. Gabriel is in trouble.
12. I meet Gabriel's friends. They are trouble, too.
13. Gabriel hurts everything, especially himself.
14. I send Gabriel to sleep-away camp. He returns as a non-human.
15. He has a new language. It is the language of fuck you.
16. In the middle of the night I ship him out.
17. In the middle of the day, fifteen months later, I bring him home.
18. Drugs. Cigarettes. Beer. Knives. Condoms. Police. Court.
19. Early in the morning, I ship him out again.
20. Death to the mother, the father, the son, and the family.
21. What do we do now?

"I'm trying to convince him to stay in Utah when he finishes high school," I say.

"I'm hoping he will find a cult and have seven wives." But the joke (it really isn't a joke) is lost on my father.

"Errrrrrrrrrrrrrrrrrrrrrrrrrrrrrrrrrrrrrrrrrr," moans the roommate.

That's it; I'm gone. A dying father, a noisy roommate, and a mother who barely speaks in a room with more lights, bells, whistles and buttons than a video game arcade, is more than I can bear for one day's penance. I kiss my father on the forehead, hug my mother, and change my mindset the moment I cross the threshold of his room.

When Paula was recuperating from surgery after her ectopic pregnancy, I spent a lot of time walking around the mall. I bought several pairs of pants, new shoes and shirts. By the time she was released I had an entirely new wardrobe. I'm not in the mood to shop right now, but a movie is not beyond the range of possibility. Maybe a double feature?

As I leave the hospital I walk through the baby loading zone. It's an oversized parking space right by the front door where the fathers of newborns can pick-up their babies and wives as they leave the hospital after birthing. A large black Cadillac Escalade, the size of a small school bus, occupies the space. An orderly is wheeling out a mother in a black wheelchair. She is plump and pretty. The father walks beside them and carries the baby, swinging him gently to and fro in a gray car seat with blue and red padding. I stop and stare at the baby, who is strapped in as securely as any NASCAR driver doing laps at Daytona. The baby is tiny, his eyes far too large for a head the size of my fist.

Then I sneeze and everyone looks at me. What do they see? They see nothing, of course, and return to putting mother and baby into the car. They are not looking at me, but I am certainly looking at them. They have an expensive car and probably a nice house with a puppy waiting in the backyard that no doubt will fall in love and protect this baby for most of its young life…until the baby outlives the dog. They have a room that is waiting for the baby. They have a crib with soft bumpers and a mobile that plays Puff the Magic Dragon as miniature birds of assorted colors spin above the baby's head. They have love and I know it is enough. How do I know this? The dying man beside my father told me. He told me through his one dying eye as I stood at the threshold revising my thinking.

I should be singing the Circle of Life from the The Lion King, but I don't. A death. A birth. A love. And what do I have? An endless love stuck in Utah with a future unknown to the speaking and the silent.

My father is not dead. Gabriel is not free. I am still lost.

Chapter 21

I really didn't know how much time I had left with Gabriel. Nothing seemed to work anymore. Even his psychologist was nervous...not for him, but for us. I felt that Gabriel was on the cusp of a monumental decision. If he continued along the same destructive path, there would be little future for him. If somehow (and believe me I didn't know how) he could just change course then maybe things would get better. I tried to influence his life, but at thirteen I was basically locked out.

I decided to take him with me to Florida on a business trip. It wouldn't be hard to get him to come and it might be fun. He would get to hang out at the hotels and join me at the Tampa Bay Rays Major League Baseball game where the owner hosted an alumni reception for Fairleigh Dickinson University, my employer.

This is what I remember from our trip. I remember that we had to drive from West Palm Beach on the east coast of Florida to St. Petersburg on the west coast. A good portion of the trip included crossing Alligator Alley through the Everglades. Alligator Alley is a long straight highway. There is not much of a view, with the exception of an occasional abandoned car.

I said to Gabriel, "What do you think happened to the people in those cars."

"What do you mean, Dad?"

"I mean, this road is called Alligator Alley for a reason. Maybe the alligators got them."

I didn't think it was possible but Gabriel latched on to that vision and insisted I drive as fast as I could. What I thought would be a little joke had frightened him. I suppose that was my intent and I told him not to worry, that I was just kidding. Yet I would be lying if I didn't admit that it gave me a bit of pleasure to know that he was still an innocent that could be frightened. In an odd sort of way it gave me hope.

The next day we went to the baseball game. What Gabriel didn't realize was that we would be sitting in the owner's suite. It's quite an experience: cushioned seats just above home plate, a big screen TV, and as much food and drink and candy as one could possibly want. Gabriel took my cell phone and called everyone he could think of. I know it's pathetic, but I think for once in my life I impressed my son. Why shouldn't a son be impressed with his dad? I didn't get to do that often.

I introduced him to the owner of the baseball team. We watched the game. We ate. Gabriel ran around the stadium. It was a great day...memorable.

When the game was over we went back to our hotel and hung out at the pool. That night we ordered room service, watched a movie in our room and played video games. In the morning, we went to a diner for breakfast and we talked about nothing, but at least we talked. Gabriel didn't eat much, but at thirteen he was already drinking coffee and smoking. Did I ever think I would allow that? Of course not, but I wasn't about to fight it. I didn't want to ruin what I thought might be the last one-on-one trip I would ever take with my eldest son. I took a picture of Gabriel in the diner. He still looked great.

●

In the time space continuum there is a point of redemption. It rests somewhere between what I believe and what I want and what I need. It is out there among every carnival balloon that was ever tethered to a child, and every child who watched his balloon disappear into a vanishing horizon. A string broke—a hand opened—a current of air blew so hard that it cut the bond between the child and the balloon. In the openness of time, in the expanse of space, that is where my redemption lies.

And then I am driving—always driving—my car, zipping past a

country landscape as Wagner's Der Fliegende Hollander blasts on the stereo. It's a movie, of course; I am in a movie and my eyes are 180 degree cameras recording the cows in the fields and the large piles of rolled hay that from a distance look like giant balls of rotting carpet the color of the earth.

In my rearview mirror I see the road behind me and the upper right quartile of my head. My one eye is the same: it's still slightly green, slightly brown, slightly speckled. But my hair is different. It's not thin and grey and fine to the touch, but black and short and brittle. When I place my hand against my scalp it feels like a thousand tiny daggers pressing their way into my palm. They are minuscule specks of pain carrying an unknown poison…a poison from Him, Her or It. The antidote is my redemption. I know it. I feel it. I see it out there somewhere among the blue sky and the green grass and a pink carnival balloon.

My breath is heavy and my heart is rising in my throat. A bead of sweat is weaving a circuitous path down my forehead. At each new wrinkle it swerves a fraction to the left and a decimal to the right until it reaches my eyebrow where I brush it aside.

I'm frightened but I'm ready. I'm alert but I'm scared. There is a giant machine with swirling blades cutting a path through the cows and carpeted fields of overgrown grass. A herd of deer, twenty or more, is drinking at a pond. One of the deer wanders off and is caught in the path of the machine. Its head is severed and it soars through the air like a poorly thrown football, wobbling end over end. It is not a dream. I see it. I smell it. I feel it. I press on the gas to escape the horror, but no matter how fast I travel, no matter how many fields I pass, the machine is always with me, threatening, cutting and bleeding. So I watch as the deer's head spins in an arc above me, its eyes shut and its mouth open as gobs of thick red blood trickle out from between its massive white teeth. The blood is falling to the ground like roasted red marshmallows that explode on contact, as one after another they burst on my speeding car. On and on and on I am bombarded by the marshmallows until finally I am able to slam on the breaks and close my eyes.

He is back; I smell him. He is sitting on a cow and smoking a cigarette. He looks good; he always looks good. Seven months in the Utah dessert has done little damage to the wonderful and natural hue of his countenance. His hair is shorter; it's nearly a crew-cut, and he has put on some weight. But he wears it well as he approaches his eighteenth birthday and me.

"Are you Him?" I ask. "Is it time?"

He drags on his cigarette for a moment and does not breathe. I have been there. I know what it's like. Remember, I think to myself. Breathe. Breathe. He holds the burning sensation in his lungs before releasing its grey smoke from his mouth and nose.

"Are you Him?" I ask again. "Is it time?"

Now he is smiling. He points a watery glance at my empty heart and says nothing. I need an answer; I need to know. Why won't he answer? These reunions are torture when all I want is a hug and some truth. How am I here again? I try one more time. Three's the charmer, the Holy Trinity of redemption and honesty.

"Are you him?" I plead. "Is it time?"

I open my eyes. The cow is gone, but the boy is not. He is wearing a bright orange sweatshirt and dark green pants. He carries a full pack on his shoulders and stands on a path in the woods. I have been here; I know this place. It's not a movie; it is my life. It's Gabriel in the wilderness. I paid to put him here. It is his wake-up call, his shock to the system, and my first real chance to save him. The marshmallows, the blood, the speeding car—all gone. This is how it happened. I was there. I remember.

●

Four sets of parents stood on a North Carolina wilderness trail waiting to be reunited with their sons and daughters. They came from Georgia, Florida, New York and our home state of New Jersey. Unlike their children, who had been brought to this place against their will, these eight adults had come willingly. For their children, the journey was different. Like Gabriel, they were awoken several hours into their sleep and left their homes with nothing more than a pair of jeans, a pair of shoes, and the shirts on their respective backs. Not true for us. We leisurely packed our clothes and toiletries, and although anxious, left with our free-will intact. The same cannot be said for Gabriel. He had a $4,000 escort bring him to this place. His free-will squelched. My screaming, violent, and ordinarily cursing adolescent left my home without a word. The escorts moved very fast and I could only imagine the shock that Gabriel must have experienced. I suppose I was in shock too, in the realization that Paula and I had done all that we could to save our son from himself.

On the road to North Carolina I realized that I was traveling the same route Gabriel must have been on seven weeks before. Gabriel wouldn't have shown it, but he must have been terrified—terrified and confused. And I, at this very moment, on this mountain path, felt the same. Like Gabriel, I had no idea what to expect. In my heart I prayed for change to take place, but I had no way of knowing if that actually would occur. And if Gabriel did change, would he have changed for the better? What if he was worse? I turned to Paula and said, "If this doesn't work, just take me out in a field and blow my brains out."

Paula had become accustomed to my catastrophic outbursts and said nothing. I knew, of course, that she was nervous too, as neither of us had any idea how we would be received once we were reunited with Gabriel. We hoped the reunion would be wonderful but, in truth, we knew better. We were excited, concerned and curious. Still, we had been warned by the wilderness counselors that Gabriel was not in the best state of mind, having just learned that he would not be coming home. He would, instead, be attending his first therapeutic boarding school.

And then there were the letters—those horrible letters that Gabriel wrote during the first few weeks away from home, starting with the first, after a few days:

> *Dear Mom and Dad,*
> *I've learned my lesson. Please pull me. I want to*
> *come home. I can't believe you did this to me. I am*

so pissed at you. I will be mad at you guys forever
if you don't come and get me. I want to kill myself.
I've learned my lesson. I miss everyone. I miss my brothers.
I want a fucking shower. I had so much planned. You
totally fucked up my life. I want my bed. I want my friends.
I've changed, I swear. Please bring me home. I worry
about so many things. I'll change. Please pull me from this
hell. If you don't I will burn down our house. When I get
out of here, all hell will be raised. I'm so depressed.
          Love,
          Gabe

    As I stood in the cool mountain air I could see in Paula the same cautious optimism that had carried her through infertility, adoption and all of our subsequent troubles. She had a warm face, and I liked looking at her. It was a bit fuller than twenty years ago when we met, but she retained her spirit, her youthfulness and her obvious intelligence. It was reassuring in an odd sort of way. She is, of course, my constant companion, but, so too, has been the misery of our lives together. And now, with so much unknown, who knew what horrors lie ahead.

    We hiked for about half an hour, until one of the counselors said, "Wait here." We were four nervous couples, aware yet uncertain of what was about to happen. With discomfort, all eyes stared down the long path, looking to see whose son or daughter was coming around the bend. And then the moment of recognition—the hugs, the tears, the instant amnesia as everyone forgot the horrors of life that brought these children to this place. These children who stole, these children who did drugs, these children who lied, drank, ignored their parents, destroyed their possessions, snuck out in the middle of the night, and caused such grief to their families. But for this instant of recognition, they were everyone's babies again, pure and innocent and desperate for the love of their parents. Each parent too, was desperate to give back that love unconditionally.

    As I watched two happy reunions in a row I was reminded of

an earlier time, of a three-year-old boy with a mop of curly red hair who, every day when I got home from work called out my name. "Daddy!" Gabriel would scream as he ran into my arms. And I would lift him up and kiss him, tickle him and blow raspberries on his belly, taking my treasure, my boy, for long walks through the suburban streets. And I could see the people that saw a father and son walking and I noticed the expressions on their faces and I felt what they were thinking, remembering how simple and lovely life could be. I was proud to be a Dad, to have this great kid, this smart and fun kid to share life with. *How cool was that*, I thought, as Gabriel and I found a spot beneath a tree on a busy corner. And we sat and watched as each car drove by. And Gabriel, with such delight, would shout out their colors: "Red! Green! White! Blue! Black!" he would scream. And I knew, absolutely, that this was perfect.

Now, a dozen years later, there was Gabriel, a few hundred feet away. He wore a bright orange sweatshirt, dark green pants, a full pack on his shoulders, and a red bandana around his head. His flaming hair burst out above the bandana like a curly mushroom. As he got closer, I could see that he was filthy with the soot and dirt of several weeks in the woods. The punk had become the mountain man, shedding his customary black attire and aura. Silver chains were replaced with beads and cordage wrapped around his neck and his wrists. He was not smiling, not even a little. It was our fourteen-year-old son, looking yet again like another slice of surrealism in the altered universe of our lives.

We approached each other slowly. Gabriel let us hug him one at a time. He said, "Hi," but did not raise his arms to hug us back. He looked at me and spit on the ground. He was angry and it was obvious.

"What up," said Gabriel.

"It's great to see you," I said, my fantasy reunion crumbling in an instant. "How are you?"

"You're sending me to boarding school," said Gabriel with little affect, spitting once again on the ground.

"Yes, we are," I said, hoping that the conversation would

improve as the day progressed.

Paula and I looked at our son. The orange sweatshirt was burned in many places -- some intentional, some not. It was covered with charcoal-colored words etched into the cloth by hot coals. Words like Live, Love, Burn, and Die. He also wrote Death Squad and I Hate Myself, and I Love Lorna, the girl he had planned to meet at the mall the day after he was taken away. She was his girlfriend and he was in love. Like all things Gabriel, it was overly intense for a boy his age. But he had plans, important plans that would never be realized with her.

It would be fifteen months before Gabriel could make any real plans again. His life would become an uncompromising set of rules enforced by men and women who firmly believed that to get along in this world meant living by the established rules of society. Rules like controlling your anger, showing respect, accepting responsibility and completing your work, especially your school work. Wilderness was a shock to Gabriel's system. It was also the beginning of a long process of self-evaluation and self-control, of learning what's important in life. The process would continue at Hidden Lake Academy, the therapeutic boarding school where we had enrolled him.

Gabriel said little as the group walked toward the campsite. He continued to spit regularly, as if to show what an absolute waste of his time the last seven weeks of his life had been.

The campsite was constructed near a stream and there were several small plywood cabins spread throughout. The cabins were a new addition for the required parental overnight after parents complained about having to spend one night in the same sleeping conditions as their sons and daughters—a tarp over your body, a sleeping bag for warmth, and a large piece of clear plastic between you and the earth.

In this setting, everything was about the earth. The parents were told that the campers learned to respect the earth and to understand that we shared the earth together. The earth was the learning laboratory. Soon, everyone understood that it was not about the earth at all. Earth was a metaphor for family. And so, as each of the campers demonstrated an earth skill they had learned, they also described, metaphorically, the elements of their families personified in the various pieces or steps of each skill.

A young blonde girl with long straw-like hair started a fire with flint and a stone and some shredded bark. Another boy, using the same bark, demonstrated the art of cordage, turning the bark into braided cord. And Gabriel, with a good deal of poise, built a trap for small animals out of a stick, a string and some flat rocks. He described in detail each step of its construction, as well as how it worked. He explained that in order to learn patience he had to create a line of five traps in a row. This task seemed simple but as everyone watched Gabriel build one trap, and as the trap fell down again and again until perfectly balanced, all could appreciate how difficult it must have been to build a row of five.

When it was done, Gabriel said, "My trap is made up of a stick, some heavy flat rocks and a string. I think my brothers are the rocks and I think my parents are the stick that holds the rocks up. And I am the string that pulls out the stick that collapses the trap." The small group applauded and as I thought about Gabriel's story, the irony of his family as a trap was not lost on me. Nor was the reality that it must have been incredibly difficult for Gabriel to attend to the task of making the trap line or braiding the bark to make the cord or starting the fire with flint and a stone, since all of the campers were required to master the same set of skills.

Fortunately, Gabriel was good with his hands, and clearly he had rehearsed his story. Although it seemed to me that his presentation, while competent, was an unemotional exercise. The next project required a bit more thought and perhaps some emotion and I wondered how Gabriel would respond. Parents and campers were instructed to go into the woods and find objects to create a family sculpture. Each sculpture would show what the family was like before and after the wilderness experience. They could be simple or complex, it didn't matter. The important thing was to identify the behavior and the change everyone hoped for.

Eleven people went into the woods to gather brambles, logs, leaves, rocks, poison ivy, broken bottles, twigs and flowers—anything that could be found and used to create a story. The lone holdout was Gabriel, who never rose from his seated position on the wet grass. As we and the other families gathered our metaphors, Gabriel sat and listened to the pleas of a counselor to get it together quickly.

It was too late. As we returned with a log, a leaf and a long bent branch, we could see our son silently crying. They were not the tears of joy that I had hoped for a few hours earlier on the trail. They were tears of desperation and it was clear to me that Gabriel had opted out. The knowledge that he was not going home, the recitation of how to build a trap, and the cold reunion with his mother and father were all he could bear for the day. I could see it in Gabriel's tear-smudged face as he watched the others piece together the wilderness junk in preparation to tell their stories.

A tall red-haired boy began to speak about a branch covered with thorns. He said, "I guess it's kind of obvious what the thorns represent."

I sat next to Gabriel and put my arm around him. I asked, "Are you okay?" "No," he said loudly, "This sucks," drawing even more attention from the others in the group.

I drew a deep breath and I remembered another letter. The last letter that Gabriel had sent before learning he was going to boarding school.

> Dear Mom and Dad,
>   It is very hard to admit the mistakes I've made and the problems I've caused. I know I've broken many things and scared my brothers very much. I know the money I stole was a bad decision. I sunk so low and became too lazy to earn money. I also must address my truancy. I understand that if I didn't come here I would probably be in detention. I am also thankful a bit about your putting me here but also mad about your taking me away from so many things. When I come home

I would like to start over with school and family
relationships. I would like to be close with you. But I
would like to have my space when I need it. And I would
still like to have my weekends for myself. I want to come
home so much and be a family. It may take me a while
but it can happen. I miss you all so much.
Love,
Gabe

Like all of Gabriel's letters it was full of conflict, the same inner turmoil that I knew he was experiencing at this very moment. The others could see it, too.

Paula said, "Gabe, Dad and I collected a bunch of stuff for our sculpture. Can you help us build it?"

Gabriel said nothing; his face said it all. He needed time to regroup his thoughts, and without a word, he simply walked away, leaving us to wonder how long his and our suffering would continue.

Fifteen months later I am sitting in the office of the director of the Ridge Creek Wilderness Academy in Georgia where Hidden Lake Academy, also of Georgia and Gabriel's therapeutic boarding school, has sent him for the fourth time. They like to send kids to the wilderness when they mess-up or need an adjustment of the mind. Four trips in fifteen months is a lot. The director is a middle-aged man with a perfectly trimmed beard. He sits at a small cluttered desk, with dozens of post-its on his computer and walls. With him is Gabriel's wilderness counselor, a thin rugged-looking woman with short wavy blonde hair parted to one side, Gabriel's newly assigned school counselor, a thirty-something man with a no-bullshit demeanor, and Gabriel's former school counselor, a sweet but sad young man, clearly disappointed by Gabriel's lack of progress. I'm standing in the doorway, somewhat amazed that all five of us fit into an office no larger than a standard corporate cubicle found in any business in America.

"You have three choices," the director said to me. "One: You can call an escort service that will be here by the end of the day and they can take Gabe to a lock-down facility in Utah. Two: If an escort can't get here today, we can call the local hospital and have Gabe admitted to the psychiatric ward until appropriate transportation is arranged. Three: You can take him home. But all of us think that's a really bad idea since you will be giving Gabe exactly what he wants. Whatever you decide, it's our feeling that he can no longer benefit from this type of wilderness program. And, since he has refused to complete Ridge Creek, they won't take him back at Hidden Lake either."

"For the last hour you've been trying to get him to sign your contract," I said. "What if he decides to sign the contract after all?"

"Based on what we have seen this morning, that's no longer an option," said the director.

No one else spoke. The question was moot and I knew it. Gabriel was not about to sign anything. His every action over the last three months had brought all of us to this point. Typical of Gabriel, he had not been the worst offender. At school he had been disrespectful to his teachers and was accused of being involved in assaulting another student, although he vehemently denied that he ever struck the boy (a year later he confessed). His worst offense, however, had little to do with his mouth or his fists. His worst offense, in the seven days that he had been back at Ridge Creek and during the prior two months at Hidden Lake Academy, was that he refused to participate in the group therapy sessions, a grievous crime in the eyes of those whose livelihood depends on a willing clientele, and who believed with genuine conviction that therapy can and will make all of us better human beings. Of course, I believed that too. But Gabriel wanted out; he wanted a chance to prove that he could function in society, and he wanted desperately for me to believe him.

I didn't think it would come to this when I'd left my home at five that morning to catch a flight to Atlanta. Over the past few weeks, as Gabriel's troubles mounted, Paula and I debated about whether or not we should bring him home. One thing we were certain about: if Gabriel did come home, it would have to be on our terms. So far, our terms were nowhere in sight.

His journey had reached a stalemate. In the few hours since I'd arrived, he had been alternately defiant and pathetic. He yelled. He cried. He shook. He tugged at his hair, his fingers and his clothes. He was given an impossible choice. At least, I am sure that is what he thought. No wonder the others who saw him that morning could only envision a more restrictive, more intensely therapeutic environment for him. What else could save this sad, lost boy?

The child I saw that morning was not crazy or emotionally troubled or even oppositionally defiant. He was the observer, the boy who joined the soccer team but was afraid to kick the ball, the boy who sat in the hallway during his six-year-old karate birthday party, afraid to be put on display or singled out, and the boy who, when asked to play football with the other neighborhood kids, offered to be the referee. I knew he was stubborn. Everyone knew he was stubborn. This was Gabe, after all. He was headstrong and determined to win this and every other battle. But did he really need a lock-down facility for refusing therapy? And was more therapy really the answer? In my world, the world of reasonable adults, I know that sometimes it's good to let others win even when you have the upper hand, and so I began to think that maybe it was time to apply that strategy to Gabriel.

But first I had to believe him; I had to trust him. Should I follow the advice of every person who had worked with him in the fifteen months since we'd sent him away; or should I go with my gut? Each one of them was an expert in adolescent behavior. Each one of them had been down this road many times before with other adolescents just like Gabriel. What did I know? I was only the father who willingly relinquished parental responsibility. My heart and my instincts told me one thing. My fear and my rational mind told me something completely different.

It all began a week earlier when we received a phone call from Todd, Gabriel's peer group counselor. On the phone with Todd was Jim, the counselor who would replace Todd in Gabriel's new peer group, and Peter, the academic director at Hidden Lake Academy. It was the three of them in a small office at a very expensive private boarding school in the hills of Northern Georgia, and Paula at our home and me in my office, forty-five miles north of Paula. Todd does most of the talking. He has a soft southern accent and a very even temperament. He says, "We've decided to drop Gabriel several peer groups. We just don't feel he can complete the program by August, given his progress to date."

Of course, we knew this was coming, but it was still difficult to hear—failure yet again.

"So when will he be done?" I asked.

"We're dropping him four peer groups, so he will be complete in May of next year."

"What happened to December?" I said.

"We just don't think he can complete the program by then," said the director. "Emotionally, Gabe is in an earlier phase and our feeling is that it will take a full year for him to get through everything."

My heart is in my stomach, imagining Gabriel's response.

I said, "Gabriel will go absolutely ape-shit when you tell him."

"We know," said Todd. "That's why we are sending him back to Ridge Creek, so that he can transition into a new peer group."

But Ridge Creek is not working this time. Gabriel enjoys it too much with no intention of going back to HLA. He is too comfortable in the woods. And to no one's surprise, he refuses to participate therapeutically. So off I go to Georgia.

Gabriel will be in the woods when I arrive. He will be brought back to the base camp building where he will be told in my presence to either get with the program or get out. Getting out does not mean going home—getting out means a lock-down facility in a place on the other side of the North American continent. My function is to reinforce the seriousness of our intentions. I am shock and awe.

Unfortunately, as I drive up to the base-camp building, a group of campers are standing around, waiting to leave for their daily trek. Among them is Gabriel, and when he sees my car I hear him say, "Hey, I think that's my Dad." So much for shock and awe.

The assemblage gathers and once again the strategy is laid out.

I listen quietly as each person in the room reiterates their conviction to the plan. Jesus Christ! Another plan! It is the child-study team from Gabriel's earlier years all over again. It is the psychologists and psychiatrists and teachers and principals and social workers and policemen—all of them searching but failing to find what it takes to reach the boy that for all his life had been described as *like no other*. Even here, as much as they try, he was still like no other. It is Mr. No Other, ready to confront yet again, a gathering of common minds brought together for the agreed upon purpose of improving his life.

Gabriel enters the room. He is wearing hiking boots, dirty khakis, a white t-shirt and a black sweatshirt. He is filthy.

"What are you doing here?" he asked me.

I say nothing and let the others speak. It was his new Hidden Lake Academy counselor, Jim, the tough guy, who did most of the talking.

"Gabe, do you know why you are here?" he asked.

"Not really," said Gabriel nonchalantly.

"You can't float through this program," Jim said. "You either make a commitment or you leave. We want you to stay. We want you to complete the program. But we need to know that your commitment to Ridge Creek and HLA is real. We need you to sign a contract with us to show us your intention to do the work."

Gabriel looked pissed. He looked at the ceiling. He looked at the walls and out the window. He looked everywhere but at the person speaking to him.

"Whatever," he said.

"Gabriel," said the tough guy. "Read the contract."

Gabriel took the contract. He smirked. He rolled his eyes. He laughed under his breath. And when he finished reading it, he folded it in half and slowly tore it to pieces. He slid the pieces back across the table to the tough guy and said as easily as if he were saying good morning, "Fuck this."

That was my cue.

"Gabriel, I want you to listen very carefully to what I have to say. Leaving the program does not mean you come home." And at this point I removed three sheets of paper from my pocket and handed them to Gabriel.

"Take a look at what I have given you. The first sheet is a lock-down program in Alabama. The second sheet is a lock-down program in Utah. The third sheet is another lock-down program, also in Utah. If you don't sign the contract and get with the program here, you will be attending one of these schools. You will have more therapy. You will have fewer freedoms. You'll come home less. You will have no sports. You will not see any girls while you are there. And by the way, in all likelihood it will be a Utah school, because what I learned yesterday is that these schools are approved by the state of New Jersey and so it won't cost me a penny to send you."

His transformation was instant. His entire body began to shake. His cavalier façade became that of a frightened boy lost in the woods. He began to cry.

"You don't understand," he said. "I can't go back to HLA. I can't switch counselors again. I'll be thrown out in two weeks. I can't do it! I can't do it! I can't stay another year! Everyone is leaving. I can't go back."

He was smacking his face with his hands. He was tugging at his hair and wiping the tears from his face. He was no longer defiant; he was simply pathetic. There was no one on his side. There was no one to hug him and say everything will be alright. Push him to the wall; it's all part of the plan. Maybe he was crazy, but what I was seeing was a boy in a hole with no way out, while those of us with the rope to help him chose this unbearable moment to leave him alone with his thoughts.

"Gabriel," I said. "You can do this. I know you can. Just suck it up and get through it. That's all it takes."

"I can't," he pleaded, his body still shaking. "I can't go back."

I asked the others to leave the room so I could talk to Gabriel in private. He was beginning to calm down, and I tried to rationalize with him.

"Gabriel, you really need to sign the contract. If you hate it here, imagine what it will be like in Utah."

"I don't care. I can't spend another year at HLA. I just won't," he said.

"Gabriel, show me that you can do well here. Show me that you can get through a couple of months at HLA without any problems. You have yet to do that! Then we can discuss whether or not you have to stay a full year. Get smart and sign the contract. Do you hear what I am saying? Just show me a few months."

I wasn't saying what I wanted to say. I wanted to be direct but I dared not. I wanted to say that I will bring him home in three months if only he can hold it together. I wanted to say that I would never keep him at HLA for another year. I needed to tell him that Paula and I discussed this before I left. I had the words, "We love you and miss you too much to keep you here any longer than was originally planned." But I couldn't say that if signing the contract was to have any meaning.

"Take me home," he begged. "Give me a chance. Let me prove to you that I am ready. I'll go to school. I'll go to therapy. I promise. You never give me a chance."

"I can't do that," I said, sticking to the plan. "I can't take that chance."

But maybe I could? Maybe it was time to place my faith in my son? Fifteen months is a long time for a boy to be away from his family. I knew he had changed, but had he changed enough? I thought about all his threats over the past few months, all the things he said he would or wouldn't do. Could he keep it together? I still wasn't sure.

When the others returned to the room, I told them that Gabriel was not ready to sign the contract. I asked if he could think about it for a few hours, knowing that he would be in a more rational state of mind when not surrounded by so many demanding people. His wilderness counselor answered quickly.

"No," she said. "He has five minutes."

It was at that point that I realized that the wilderness camp and the school had done all that they could for Gabriel. They tried, they absolutely tried, but they also gave up, avoiding any real struggle that might grow out of Gabriel's staying any longer. They lived in a world of black and white; they had to. There was too much grey in the children they worked with to begin to make exceptions. Eventually, all of the children conform or are pulled by their parents or dismissed by the school. In some children, the children like Gabriel, the shades of grey are far too complex for them to ever fit in. They were the square pegs that refuse to slide into the circular holes. Part of me admired that piece of my son, but most of me resented it.

I stepped out of the room with the wilderness director and listened to what he had to say. The choices as he described them were painful, but my mind was made up. I called Paula and told her my decision. She agreed, perhaps reluctantly. I also called our educational consultant, and told her too. And then I told the assemblage.

"If it's an escort he needs, I can just as easily have one come to my home as come to this place," I said. "I am taking him home and making my decision there."

I walked back to the room where Gabriel was waiting. He looked like crap. His face was smeared from dirt and tears. His hair, long, curly and wild, has been pulled in every direction and looked it. He was sullen, frightened and confused.

"You lose," I said, with as much parental authority as I could muster. "I want to make it very clear that this is not a victory for you." I caught my breath and added angrily, "Either way, I am taking you home. You will live in my house, under my rules. You will not hang out with your friends. You will not go on the Internet. You will get a job. You will go to school. You will go to counseling." I take another long, deep breath and continue. "If you fuck-up, you will find yourself in Utah very, very quickly."

He tries to say something, but I won't let him. "Can you do this?" I asked, my voice beginning to crack, "because there isn't a single person in the state of Georgia that thinks you can."

"Yes," he said, full of emotion. "You know that is all I ever wanted. I just want to come home."

"Okay," I said. "Then let's get out of here."

And we did. And life was lovely for a brief time. And school resumed. And the cigarettes reappeared. And the cursing began anew. And the monster returned. And Gabriel reminded me that I was a pussy and Paula was a fucking bitch. And I hated the probation officer. And I despised the judge. And it wasn't like it was before. It's worse and hopeless and we were broke and broken. And twenty-two months later it takes three men two hours and a set of handcuffs to get him out of my house and bring him to Utah where they tell me it is unlikely they can change him during the seven months and $63,000 I will spend before he turns eighteen and walks out the door.

But I close my eyes and I see his deliverance. In a field, on a cow, in a car, on the beach; he is ubiquitous to my soul. And I pray to the One who does not speak to me. I ask the ever so invisible for forgiveness and guidance for both of us. I look for that space where the shallow pleading of my prayers reside. I'm always looking, always searching. But here's the thing; he's coming home. It is more than his deliverance; it is his delivery. He is making plans. He is scared and worried and free. I am scared and worried and trapped. The honeymoon is over. Lock the doors. Hide the keys (and the jewels). Reunions suck and so does redemption. Here we go again.

Chapter 22

I have been wrong about many things but mostly I have been wrong about the big It ... the He or She or He/She God-like Deity that has yet to reveal its very nature to me or embrace my own ambiguity. Yet today, as I make my way north from exit 9 to exit 13A, on the very straight and very wide and very fast New Jersey Turnpike, past massive white cylinders filled with oil soon to be converted into gasoline and other petroleum bi-products, I see for the first time the symmetrical continuity that is my life.

It's raining. No, not just raining, but pouring. It's as if the Atlantic Ocean has lifted itself from the dark and cold embrace of the continental shelves and floated like an enormous watery spaceship over the state of New Jersey. And there, held motionless by an asexual Almighty, it darkens every corner of the Garden State until, like the great walls of Jericho, the waters come crashing down, filling the open space between the earth and everything above it.

I am in the car with Paula. We are on our way to Newark Liberty International Airport to pick up Gabriel who is returning from six months at the lock-down therapeutic high school in Utah where miraculously he has graduated. I am reminded of another trip, another storm, another section of the New Jersey Turnpike, where Paula and I traveled nearly 18 years ago to witness the birth of our son. I remember what I said as the rain slammed against the car and I struggled nervously to maintain control. I said, "It's a test. If we survive the storm, if we make it to the hospital alive, then everything will be all right. It's just another test."

Wrong; it wasn't a test at all, it was a sign, another sign from Him, Her or It. *There's a bigger storm brewin', young fella. Are you ready? Can you handle it?*

I am watching the lightening on the horizon as I drive to the

186

airport. Each flash is long and jagged and reflects against the raindrops like a slow strobe light. And I count...one, two, three, four...ka-boom! Four miles until we reach the lightening—ten miles until we reach our destination.

We can only laugh, living a history that is so obviously repeating itself. Another flash off in the distance...one, two, three, four, five... ka boom! The storm is moving away, yet we are getting closer to its message.

Thump. Thump. Thump. Thump. Thump. "What the hell is that," I say to Paula. "Did you hear that?"

I pull over as the water continues to pound us from above. It feels and looks like hail, but it's not. It is the enormous weight of an onslaught of super-sized raindrops that is hammering New Jersey.

In the midst of the pounding faux hail, I step outside the car and inspect my tires as other cars, their nervous drivers clinging to their steering wheels, whiz by me. We have a flat. We are stuck. We are being pummeled from the heavens above, and as if that isn't enough, our mode of transportation has been crippled. Could the message be any clearer? *Turn around, Rick. Turn around quickly!*

And all I can think of is that Gabriel is going to be so pissed if we are late to pick him up. He's got plans, bank on it. It's Sunday night, after all, and he's back after six months on the road...lots of catching up to do. And then I realize, of course, that no plane is landing in this mess. He will be as late as we are.

So we wait. We call for a service to change the tire. We laugh at life's little ironies. We call the airline (to absolutely no avail) and try to get a message to Gabriel. And we never never never say that which is so incredibly obvious to two people whose lives have not just been peppered with sadness and madness and little bits of horror, but whose very gestalt is unyielding pain of the heart. And the tire is fixed. And the rain stops. And the sun comes out. And the steam is rising from the New Jersey Turnpike taking with it the memory of another wet and wild day. And off we go to pick up our son again.

There he is. I see him. He is standing outside the terminal with a large burgundy duffle bag. His hair is short, really short. I pull up to the curb. Paula gets out of the car and gives Gabriel a hug. I open my door. I walk around the car and approach him. "Hi, Gabe," I say, as I wrap my arms around him and squeeze him tight. I smell him and he is clean, not overcome by the scent of nicotine. I feel him and he is heavier but not overweight. And I kiss him on the neck. I do it once and then I instantly do it again, as my entire body becomes overwhelmed by an emotion I had mostly not associated to him in a very long time. There is a dryness in my mouth. There is a weight in my throat. And there is an accumulation of moisture building in my eyes. And then I release him, knowing as I always have that whatever this emotion means to me, it may mean nothing to him, and so I let it pass.

I know I am cynical and I wish that I wasn't. I wish I could look at my beautiful boy with the same eyes that held him on the day of his birth when all my dreams seemed fulfilled, when I would not hesitate for a second to weep out of joy. It's like trying to remember Muhammad Ali when he could speak and move with ease. He smiles…that's all I need. He flashes a stinging jab…that's all I want. It's vivid and distant and incredibly far away. Yet here he is, no further than a breath.

We load the car and begin to drive south. South is the direction of the abductors. Wilderness—boarding school—lock down—home…we are heading home. We will never send him away again. That is my promise.

His brothers are thrilled to see him. First they take him to his new basement room to show him the new dresser and the long wooden bar that I hung from the ceiling where he can hang his shirts and jackets. They bounce on the bed that we have put there, and they show Gabriel all the new video games that he can play on the television beside his bed. I think that Gabriel likes the basement set-up; he's certainly not complaining.

Then they take him to my room, which was formerly Gabriel's room, which is now my study. I am surprised that he doesn't give me any grief for relegating his life to the basement. "You got a flat screen T.V.," he says with enthusiasm, referring to the fifteen inch

T.V. that rests on my desk.

"Yeah, I did," I respond.

"That's so cool."

Is this the new Gabriel? Is this the new cocktail of meds that actually works? Or is it simply hour number one, with thousands and thousands of hours to come. I refuse to accept anything on face value. His normalcy doesn't fool me, not one bit.

Rule number 1:	Curfew is 1:00 a.m.
Rule number 2:	No smoking on or near our property
Action number 1:	Key locks on all bedroom doors.
Action number 2:	No keys for Gabriel

That's it. That's our plan. It's not a fresh start. It's not forgiveness. It's safety for us, for Gabriel, for the boys. Give him what he wants. Get him a job. Get him out of the house. We are fully immersed in maintenance mode.

By 9:00 p.m. (he was home for about two hours) he is gone. That is his plan. He has gone from boarding school to boarding room. He has graduated from dozens of rules and restrictions to two. He is basically on his own as he ritualistically begins his immersion into the universe of high school graduates of which he is inexplicably one. He is a bit like Moses, who after murdering the Egyptian leaves Egypt to become a shepherd in a foreign land. Years later he returns to confront his brother, the Pharaoh, armed with a new attitude, a new mission, and yes, a few new weapons... the Entity/Deity covering his back.

So I ask myself, *is he different?* And the answer, of course, is no, not yet. He is excited to be home. He jokes with me and his brothers. He is not cursing. He is not smoking. He is not stealing. He is not threatening. But, come on, it's only been two hours.

"I'm afraid," I say to Paula, "that all we did was put off the inevitable."

"Maybe," she says, "but maybe all we needed was some time away from each other to break the awful pattern that had become our lives. You expect too much."

That evening, Gabriel is home by midnight, regaling stories of so many reunions.

The next day, I take him shopping and give him a new cell phone. That night he doesn't get home until 1:20 a.m. At 1:10 I lock the doors and don't let him in until 2:30 when he sends me a text message which says, "Please let me come in."

I tell him we're serious about his curfew and he tells me under his breath to go fuck myself. What's most interesting, however, is that during the hour and ten minutes he was locked-out of the house, he made absolutely no fuss at all. He sat on the porch and patiently waited for my empty heart to give in.

The next day, when I come home from work, he has shaved his head. It freaks me out having a skin-head in the family, but I deal with it. He claims that being in the Utah sun dried out his hair and he has every intention of letting it grow back. That night he goes to the Jersey Shore with his friends and does not come home until the following day. At 1:30 in the morning he calls me on my cell phone to tell me he lost track of time. I tell him not to bother coming home and he is fine with that. I am ready to kill him, even though he called and even though I know where he is…sort of.

When he comes home the next day, I can smell the cigarette smoke that engulfs him. Okay, that was expected. What wasn't expected was the large silver cross around his neck. Very nice, indeed! (Jewish, in case you forgot.) My desire to cause him pain is increasing exponentially.

Paula is philosophical. We're only an hour from the shore and all the kids go there over the summer. This is true, but all the other kids are not like Gabriel. Lest we forget that he is *like no other.*

"These are baby steps," I tell Paula. "He is slowly inching his way back to his old life. How can you not see it? How can you be so goddamn naïve," I tell her emphatically. And the next day he is home by eight and his friends hang out and watch videos in Gabriel's basement pad.

And the next day he is home by nine and his friends hang out again.

And the next day he comes home at 12:55 a.m.

And the next day he and one of his friends bring home two gorgeous young girls and they watch a movie in the basement. They take the girls home at 10:00 p.m. and Gabriel is back by 1:00. And I think he is into his basement with all the accoutrements of an apartment, even though Mom and Dad are two flights above him and there is no lock on his door.

And a week has gone by and there has not been a single act of violence, nothing is missing, there has only been some mild cursing, and yes, he is still an incredible slob, but who really cares about the basement anyway.

And he is up until two or three in the morning, just like the good old days. And he is smoking in the bathroom, (I see the ashes in the garden below the bathroom window.) and when he woke up at 11:30 this morning he cleaned his room.

I say to him, "If you continue to smoke in the bathroom, I am going to throw you out of the house when you're eighteen." (only a few weeks away)

"I'm not fucking smoking in the bathroom," he says.

"I'm not kidding," I say and I walk away.

Outside the house, I'm bringing in the trash cans, and at the end of the driveway I find a cigarette butt: Marlboro. It's just another adorable baby step to hell. That's what I think. So I walk back inside, the filthy one and half inch butt held deftly between my thumb and index finger. I approach Gabriel who is sitting at my desk, typing on my computer.

"Give me your hand," I say, as I grab his wrist and turn his palm toward heaven. At the moment that the cup of his hand becomes parallel to the horizon, I take the cigarette butt, held firmly in my other hand, and grind it into the spot at the center of his palm where his life lines cross. And once again I walk away. And once again he does nothing, not even an obligatory fuck you.

I am baffled by his control, and because I am baffled I can't stay angry very long. The truth is that I like having him around.

I take comfort in the fantasy of a family that is whole, although I hold no illusion that this fantasy will last any more than another day, another hour, another minute. It was hard when we were only four fifths, hard to look at those family pictures from Jonathan's Bar Mitzvah—a handsome family of four, one child missing.

I may not believe in God anymore but I do want to believe that Gabriel has a soul. So here is my proof: a letter that he sent to Jonathan just before he left Utah.

> *Dear Jonathan,*
>
> *What's good bro? By the time you get this letter I'll be home but there is something I want you to know. First of all I love you and Ethan to death. These last six months waking up and not having fun with you has been hard. As a big brother I have a responsibility to be there for the younger ones. I feel I have failed that from since I was 14 until now. I haven't been there physically to take care of you and watch over you when Mom and Dad weren't around. I really broke down after I heard I missed your Bar Mitzvah. It really killed me hard. Still thinking about it makes me tear while writing this letter. All I could think about was how the whole family was there except your own brother and how I can never go back in time and do that day all over again. All I hope is that day you were happy and felt your family and friends warmth. Life has been a journey Jonathan and I have gone through so much, you can't even imagine. I will, one day, when you're older, tell you all the bad I have seen so you're ready to face it and know the real dangers of the world. I'm still learning but already I learned so much. I know you and Ethan have seen some scary stuff when I've been mad. Anger is strange with me (it's something I don't get) but I've gotten better with it. I never liked scaring the family. I'd rather be close to you than far away. Remember Grandpa's funeral? I sure do. Me*

and you cried like little babies. I could only think about
how I lost so many chances to spend time with him and
how much I miss him. When me and you were crying I
remember holding you in my arms and I felt so close to
you and knew that I wanted to stay close with my family
and do good. All in all, what I am saying is that you're
my brother and I love you and Ethan no matter what I
have to overcome. I'm so proud of you.
    Love,
    your Bro, Gabriel

THE END

Postscript

By Paula Kalpan-Reiss, Ph.D.

I am not the writer. My husband is the writer. He is the creative, literary one who has spun our *challenging* lives into a tale of horror, humor, despair and hope, all with incredible honesty. I am the clinical psychologist. I have been asked to use my years of experience, both professional and personal, to offer wisdom and insight for those who may be having similar struggles. I am here to say that despite being well-educated, financially comfortable and in a solid marriage, life can still go so wrong. But, I can also say there are some ways, some resources, some tools which can help make life more bearable for everyone.

Ironically, while a graduate student, I worked extensively with adjudicated delinquent males who were mandated to in-home family therapy in rural, impoverished Appalachia. I would marvel at how most of these youths cared little for the significant distress they were causing their parents. Had they no empathy for their mothers and fathers? An idea for a master's thesis and doctoral dissertation was born. I would assess the affective empathy and cognitive role-taking skills of these teens and then develop an intervention to improve these skills, along with their moral reasoning skills in a population of incarcerated delinquent males. For 10 weeks, along with my grad assistants, I made the 75-mile trek to the nearest prison to supervise these groups. Not surprisingly, my intervention was unsuccessful. Despite my naïve hopes and my best efforts, I could not turn these youths into caring, empathic, reasonable human beings. Along the way, I decided this was not a population with whom I cared to work in the future.

Still interested in working with children, adolescents and families, I chose an internship after graduate school that would provide training with these populations. As an intern, I worked with many youths diagnosed with Attention Deficit Hyperactivity Disorder (ADHD). My supervisor loved these kids. Consequently, I conducted many assessments and worked with several families under his guidance. Again, I thought, *I'm not loving this work.*

Then, I experienced years of infertility and miscarriage, culminating in our decision to adopt Gabriel. Every program I attended on adoption featured new parents blissfully in love with their new babies, grateful to put an end to their childless years of longing and misery. And, adopting Gabriel did make a huge difference, both personally and professionally. I experienced complete euphoria as a new mother to my beautiful son. Plus, I discovered a niche in the world of therapy where I felt I could make my mark. I would counsel others experiencing infertility and expose them to all the options available to create a family. I dove into this work, running groups, giving lectures, attending workshops, reading everything I could find. I connected with other adoption and infertility professionals; I joined an adoptive family playgroup. I had found my calling.

Who knew that my personal and professional life would collide with the world of ADHD and juvenile delinquency? The prospective and adoptive parents I now worked with or I befriended in my private life were nothing like the poor, uneducated families in Ohio. Arrogantly, I believed the parents I knew were not lacking in the parenting skills needed for children who may have behavioral, neurological or cognitive *issues*.

ADOPTION: What they don't tell you

Most parents who pursue adoption, in particular those who have endured numerous failed procedures and miscarried pregnancies, are eager to get a baby in their arms and join the world of happy families. Adoption can provide that. We see every celebrity walking around with a newly rescued infant, often from a developing nation, usually of a different race. We admire these celebrities for using their wealth to parent a child who most certainly would not have grown up with the comforts of a family who can provide the best of everything. These children look healthy, well cared for and happy.

But these adorable babies and toddlers grow up, and while many may do well, their parents are often not prepared for the difficulties they may face. As a group, research shows that adopted children are two to three times more likely to have adjustment difficulties including: delinquency, school problems and behavioral disorders than nonadopted children (Keyes et al., 2008; Reuter & Koerner, 2008). Of course, there are many reasons offered for these statistics, but, the point is, adoptive parents are rarely educated about problems their children may experience as they develop. The message is *nurture trumps nature*. Very few parents are told how powerful a role nature and genetics can play. Parents hope their adopted children will be healthy and happy. They may have little access to the genetic or health history of the biological parents. They may dismiss a history of ADHD as not being significant or one they can easily manage with supportive teachers, a structured environment or medication. Yet, ADHD can predispose children to significant academic struggles, social problems and difficulties with impulsivity which can have wide-reaching implications.

Prospective adoptive parents need as much access to genetic and family history as possible and need a realistic depiction by adoption professionals of what their lives may look like past the adorable stages of infancy and toddlerhood. Adoption education must be more thorough and comprehensive. Parents need much more support through the tumultuous years of adolescence, long after the adoption agency fades into the background, years after the adoption is finalized. When I discussed my concerns with Adam Pertman, Executive Director of the Evan B. Donaldson Adoption Institute, he said they were moving in the direction of creating training sessions for adoptive parents. Along with Dr. David Brodzinsky, a noted psychologist and researcher in the field of adoption, they have developed a curriculum which I hope will become as essential as the home study for parents who plan to adopt.

SUPPORT GROUPS

When Gabriel was little, I connected with other adoptive parents, mostly through our local chapter of RESOLVE: The National Infertility Association, and we formed a playgroup. While other new mothers shared child birth stories, issues with nursing and when to plan to conceive their next child, we would talk about contact with birth families, what agencies or attorneys we used and how we were going to share our stories of our children's adoption with them. I loved our play group and delighted in our children all playing with each other just as children did in other play groups. Having the support of other parents who share a similar experience can be invaluable to feeling understood and supported. When our children were too old for play groups, I had an adoption holiday party every year. The same parents brought their children. We ate, opened presents, celebrated the holidays; our children played, never discussed their adoption, but knew the reason they were brought together. Gabriel loved these parties. As Gabriel's behavior escalated out of control, the parties ended, but my contact with other parents did not. I learned I was not alone with my challenges. Ten years later, although not in touch with all the parents, here is what I know about our play group: Another boy was sent to wilderness for pulling a knife on his mother; one girl left home one day after *hooking up* with an older boy (with a criminal history) at a party, got pregnant, married him and virtually never contacts her parents because he won't *allow* it; another boy has severe Asperger's Syndrome and a history of violence and was sent to live in a residential program; one girl struggles academically and was sent to a school for children with learning disabilities; another girl, despite a high IQ, has struggled to perform academically, suffers from ADHD, and has had a very difficult relationship with her parents, but is unsure of her academic future or career plans. And my experience is not unique. My friend, a therapist, whom I first went to hear speak when I was exploring adoption, who advised me on wilderness and boarding school programs because her son had also attended, told me half her original adoption playgroup had been in residential treatment.

The bottom line is, we need support. Most of us did not grow up in an environment filled with extreme academic, behavioral and legal trouble. While we may be educated, we are clueless as to how to navigate the worlds in which we now live. We imagine other parents judging our parenting for having children so out of control. We need to connect with comrades who are engaged in similar *wars*. For those who have few personal connections to other troubled parents, the Internet can bring this population to your desktop and help with the feeling of isolation. There are sites for those experiencing infertility, for parents of adopted children, children who have attended residential and wilderness programs, and parents of children suffering from various mental health issues.

PROFESSIONALS

While friends are critical, we cannot manage without a team of professionals who can intervene and provide guidance. Typically, we learn this is necessary the first time our children enter school. When behavioral and academic concerns are noted, someone, usually a school psychologist needs to do a thorough evaluation of your child's academic, cognitive and social skills. We were always fortunate to have an ally in our school who worked very hard to get the services we needed for Gabriel. One reason I believe we were able to do so was our approach in working with the school, enlisting the empathy of the case manager and keeping in close contact with teachers and administrators. Seeing the school's number pop up on my caller ID was always enough to induce nausea. However, I knew there was someone I could call who would intervene and be understanding of my distress and my son's out of control behavior.

When pursuing wilderness and residential settings, having an experienced educational consultant can help navigate the numerous programs of varying quality which are out there. An old friend of my parents whom I had not seen since childhood was a wonderful consultant. She was the liaison between us and these programs and proved invaluable.

Being in the field of mental health, finding a good therapist (who was not a friend or colleague) was of paramount importance. Getting Gabriel to go to therapy (or anywhere, for that matter) was no easy task. However, even when Gabriel refused to go, I, and sometimes Rick and I needed someone to talk to. Therefore, the therapist we found for Gabriel needed to be someone with whom we could communicate as well. While checking credentials and experience is important, several other issues are necessary to examine when making a choice. Has the therapist had good success working with other boys with adoption issues, ADHD, and Oppositional Defiant Disorder? Is the therapist aware of available resources in the community that might benefit your child? How does the therapist handle crises or talk to your child when he is out of control? What was probably most critical for us, however, was when our therapist told us: we should call the police when we felt in danger; it may not be safe to have Gabriel live with us any longer; it was time to explore a residential setting. While this is painful to consider, is often a last resort, and usually requires significant financial resources, parents need to realize when they can no longer manage their children at home, especially when there may be younger siblings in the house. Nothing is more difficult than having to send away a child who was adopted—who has already been *given away* by their biological parents. But, sometimes, there are just no other options.

Finding a good psychiatrist, as well, may provide some relief from the symptoms of ADHD, rage and depression. We were less successful in this arena, not because we could not find good physicians, but we were unable to find the right combination of meds which made a significant difference in improving Gabe's mood and behavior. It was not for lack of trying. Gabriel took many of the newer antidepressants and anti-anxiety medications, anti-psychotics and stimulants that were available with varying degrees of side effects and minimal success. When he was around 11, he experienced severe anxiety and was prescribed one of the SSRI's (serotonin reuptake inhibitors) which he described as making him feel fearless. While we were grateful for his decrease in anxiety, our worries only increased as Gabe felt less of a need to curb any risk-taking impulses. The stimulants did make him more attentive in school, but we experienced the fall-out at home when the medication wore off. Fortunately, improvements in these meds are developing all the time and we continue to search for a drug which may be helpful.

MARRIAGE AND FAMILY

How many times I have been asked, *How has your marriage survived this? My husband and I would have been divorced by now!* While marriages can definitely experience a strain during extreme conflict, while there can be little time for fun and romance when fires must constantly be extinguished, I have always maintained that crises highlight all the kinks already present in a relationship and do not necessarily create new ones. Any personality flaws you may have been able to keep under control during peaceful times will likely rear their heads under extreme stress. Certainly, Rick and I have our share of flaws and differences. But, fortunately, we created a solid foundation based on shared values and interests during our courtship and our early marriage. At the same time, we were fairly actualized separate human beings with strong identities going into parenthood. Rick had solid career aspirations, creative pursuits and a major interest in physical fitness which I supported. I, too, felt strongly about my profession, had a passion for the arts, and also worked hard to stay in shape. During all we endured, we made time to keep all these interests alive. Of course, this required a strong ability to compartmentalize, at which we both became quite proficient. Rarely, were we both in a state of despair at the same time. When Rick could no longer tolerate Gabe's anger and rage,

200

I was often able to feel empathy. When I was constantly feeling terrorized, Rick would step in and manage Gabe. We tried to be *on the same page* with how we wanted to respond to Gabe's behavior. We avoided blaming each other when we lost control (as we often did) or when we failed to be consistent with our expectations. Both times we made the decision to send Gabe away, we made sure to come to that decision together. Often times, however, we did not come to that decision at the same time and we had to wait for the other to come around.

We love to entertain and we continued to do so, taking refuge in being with good friends and reassuring ourselves that we were good people caught in an often unmanageable situation. We still went out to dinner and went to the movies, or Rick would sit and write while I would sit and read in another room. We tried to hold onto who we were when we could control little else.

Having other children at home was both a blessing and an added stress. We felt lucky to have another more *normal* experience at parenting, if, for no other reason than to enable us to believe we could be good parents with children who were by no means perfect, but, basically acted like they loved us and wanted to be with us. However, witnessing Gabe's out of control behavior as parents was difficult enough. Having our other children bear witness to the chaos, and at times be victim to Gabriel's violence felt unacceptable. They were often afraid and looked to us to make them feel safe. While we might have been able to put up with Gabe's behavior at home, we knew we could not expect the same from his younger siblings. When Gabriel was away, we needed to heal. And, eventually, with time, our lives took on some semblance of normalcy.

Unfortunately, not everyone has a spouse with whom they can share parenting or a loving supportive relationship. And, other parents may not get the chance to parent another child who does not present constant challenges. Hopefully, family members can be a comforting and understanding presence. We both have close siblings who love Gabe unconditionally, yet understand the horrors we have experienced and are often available to listen. My mother, in particular, has been a constant ear. While she has been the parent of three successful children, she quickly became well versed in the troubles we faced. Because she lives far away, and we do not see each other often, she has been able to see the subtle changes and improvements Gabe has been able to make over the years. She is an outside observer who has been able to shed a light of hope. She can see when he is exhibiting kindness, or empathy, or remorse. She has also witnessed his worst behavior and has been able to feel both compassion for him and his impulses, and for us in our inability to deal with him. She does not judge and we are so grateful.

I wish I had more I could offer parents who are struggling with a difficult child whom they love but cannot manage. My experience, both personal and professional, often has not felt like enough. Love has not been enough to help Gabriel make the strides we hope for him. But, love of my husband, my family and my friends has sustained me. The professionals we have met along the way have provided the support. The lives we hope to touch with our story give us added hope and purpose. Ultimately, we dream of a day when Gabriel can use all the love, support, resources and education that surround him to live a full, productive and, most importantly, peaceful life.

Acknowledgements

In the beginning Paula said, "You should really send this to The Times." So I did. Thank you, Paula, for having faith in my writing, for making a wonderful suggestion, for being a terrific editor and for being at my side, now and forever. You are the bravest person I know. Thank you Dan Jones of *The New York Times* for publishing *Sending a Lost Boy Into the Wilderness to Find Himself*. Were it not for you, Anna Stein would have never asked me the following question: "Have you ever thought about writing a book?" Thank you, Anna, for your suggestion, and for your guidance during the early development of *Desperate Love*. And thank you, Susan Ramer, for your later guidance and for convincing me I still had something worth publishing.

Thank you to everyone in the MFA Program in Creative Writing at Fairleigh Dickinson University, especially the wonderful Thomas E. Kennedy who encouraged me and challenged me and helped me to find my voice.

In the end, this memoir would never have come together were it not for the many talents of Cindy Paul, who generously agreed to take a fine tooth comb to my words and helped me to make sense out of the story I was trying to tell.

To Gabriel, despite the difficulties you continue to face and despite the awful things I have said in angst, I still love you deeply. And to Ethan and Jonathan, I hope that when you are older you will understand why I wrote this book and that you might forgive me for sharing the truth about our family.

Finally, this memoir might still be collecting dust in cyberspace were it not for the generous hearts of the folks at Serving House Books, specifically Walter Cummins and Thomas E. Kennedy. Thank you for hearing my voice and for believing that what I had to say—and the way in which I said it—might make a difference to someone somewhere.

Richard Reiss began his professional writing career at the *Piscataway-Dunellen Review*, a Forbes newspaper, for which he wrote and was recognized by the New Jersey Press Association for his humor column, *Reiss's Pieces*. Over the next twenty five years he developed his skills as a professional fundraiser working primarily for colleges and universities. During that period he also wrote extensively about creating a family through adoption, and the joys and challenges of being adoptive parents. His writings have appeared in *The New York Times*, *ADDitude Magazine*, *Perigee Literary Journal*, and in the anthology, *Upstart Crows II: True Stories*, published by Wide Array Press. In 2008 Reiss collaborated with director and lyricist Martin Charnin to create the musical revue *Love is Love*. He is a lifetime resident of New Jersey where he lives with his wife and three children.

Paula Kaplan-Reiss, Ph. D., has been a licensed psychologist in the state of New Jersey for over 20 years. Specializing in adoption, infertility and loss, she has written and lectured extensively on these topics for both parents and professionals. She received her undergraduate degree from Cornell University and received her doctorate from Ohio University.

Cover Artist

Elyse Rosenberg received a Bachelor of Fine Arts from the University of Michigan–Ann Arbor, with a major in Graphic Design and a minor in Painting. She received a Masters in Art Education from Maryland Institute College of Art. She has showcased her work in a number of venues, including the Abington Art Center in Abington, PA, Salt and Pepper in Philadelphia, PA, and Willow Restaurant in Arlington, VA. Her works include paintings, relief prints, and mixed media collages. She currently resides in New York City where she teaches Visual Art to middle school students in a Bronx public school.